The Many Phases of Matter

Vignettes in Physics
A Series by G. Venkataraman

Published
The Many Phases of Matter
Why Are Things the Way They Are?
Bose and His Statistics
Chandrasekhar and His Limit
A Hot Story
At the Speed of Light
The Quantum Revolution (3 vols.)
1. The Breakthrough
2. QED: The Jewel of Physics
3. What is Reality?
Raman and His Effect
Bhabha and His Magnificent Obsessions
Saha and His Formula

Forthcoming
The Big and The Small

Vignettes in Physics

The Many Phases of Matter

G. Venkataraman

Universities Press

THE MANY PHASES OF MATTER

UNIVERSITIES PRESS (INDIA) PRIVATE LIMITED

Registered Office
3-6-747/1/A & 3-6-754/1, Himayatnagar, Hyderabad 500 029, Telangana, India
info@universitiespress.com; www.universitiespress.com

Distributed by
Orient Blackswan Private Limited

Registered Office
3-6-752 Himayatnagar, Hyderabad 500 029, Telangana, India

Other Offices
Bengaluru / Chennai / Guwahati / Hyderabad / Kolkata
Mumbai / New Delhi / Noida / Patna

First published 1991
Reprinted 1993, 1997, 2011, 2014, 2022, 2024

ISBN 978-81-7371-034-6

502031

Typeset by
Texi Toolers, Hyderabad 500 001

Printed in India by
B B Press,
Tronica City, Ghaziabad, U.P. 201103

Published by
Universities Press (India) Private Limited
3-6-747/1/A & 3-6-754/1, Himayatnagar, Hyderabad 500 029, Telangana, India

The design of the cover is a computer pattern generated by G. Athithan. For details see Chapter 3.

Contents

Preface

To the adult reader

This book and others in this series written by me are inspired by the memory of my son Suresh who left this world soon after completing school. Suresh and I often used to discuss physics. It was then that I introduced him to the celebrated *Feynman Lectures.*

Hans Bethe has described Feynman as the most original scientist of this century. To that perhaps may be added the statement that Feynman was also the most scintillating teacher of physics in this century.

The Feynman Lectures are great but they are at the textbook level and meant for serious reading. It seemed to me that there was scope for small books on diverse topics in physics which would stimulate interest, making at least some of the young students take up later a serious study of physics and reach for the Feynman as well as the Landau classics.

Small books inevitably remind me of Gamow's famous volumes. They were wonderful, and stimulated me to no small extent. Times have changed, physics has grown and we clearly need other books, though written in the same spirit.

In attempting these volumes, I have chosen a style of my own. I have come across many books on popular science where elaborate sentences often tend to obscure the scientific essence. I have therefore opted for simple English, and I don't make any apologies for it. If a simple style was good enough for the great Enrico Fermi, it is also good enough for me. I have also employed at times a chatty style. This is deliberate. Feynman uses this with consummate skill, and I have decided to follow in his footsteps (whether I have succeeded or not, is for readers to say). This book is meant to be read for fun and excitement. It is a book you can even lie down in bed and read. Without going to sleep I hope!

Naturally I have some basic objectives, the most important of which is to stimulate the curiosity of the reader. Here and there the reader may fail to grasp some details, and in fact I have deliberately pitched things a bit high on occasions. But if the reader is able to experience at least in some small measure the *excitement* of science, then my purpose would

Nature into different subjects, she herself knows no such boundaries. So we can always start anywhere, take a random walk and catch a good glimpse of Nature's glory. Where she is concerned, all topics are 'fashionable'. There is today an unnecessary polarization of the young towards subjects that are supposed to be fashionable. To my mind this is unhealthy, and I have tried to counter it.

This series is essentially meant for the curious. With humility, I would like to regard it as some sort of a 'Junior Feynman Series', if one might call it that. With much love, and sadness, it is dedicated to the memory of Suresh who inspired it.

To the young reader

This book is about phase transitions. You probably haven't heard the term before. It denotes a change of state like, for example, water becoming steam. People are interested in phase changes for many reasons. For instance, metallurgists are keen to know the properties solids have in their various possible phases. This is because they are always on the lookout for better materials, and they would like to know if there exist phase transitions which would lead them to better materials.

Physicists are interested in phase transitions for a different reason. They want to know *why* such transitions occur, and whether there is anything common between the numerous transitions that one observes in Nature. When one begins asking such questions, one can truly wander all over the place! I shall be taking you through one such tour in this book. Pleasant reading!

Acknowledgements

The idea for a series such as this was first suggested to me by Dr. V.G. Kulkarni of the Homi Bhaba Centre for Science Education, to whom I am very grateful. Mr. John D. Vincent gave me invaluable help in getting access to reference material. Particular thanks are due to Professors V. Balakrishnan, N. Mukunda and Ajay Sood for a careful scrutiny of the manuscript and for making various critical observations. Mr. G. Athithan has kindly provided the computer output of Penrose tilings, while Dr. V.S. Raghunathan supplied the electron diffraction picture of a quasi crystal. Mrs. Naga Nirmala has rendered very useful assistance in the preparation of the manuscript. It has been a pleasure to work with Universities Press the publisher, and their friendly cooperation is much appreciated.

G.VENKATARAMAN

1 *What Is A Phase?*

When ice melts it becomes water, and when water is heated to the boiling point, it becomes steam. Everybody knows this. We also know about the reverse processes namely, steam condensing into water and water freezing into ice. You may have learnt that in ice the water molecules are neatly arranged in a lattice (Fig. 1.1), and that when ice is warmed, the molecules become restless, rattle around a bit till they break loose, and then start wandering all over, rather like a young person leaving home to explore the wide world. This is one way of describing melting. The change of a liquid into vapour can be described in similar terms (see Box 1.1).

Ice, water and steam all contain the same molecule H_2O and yet they are strikingly different. You may say, 'That ought to be. After all, ice is a solid, water is a liquid and steam is a vapour'. True, but there is another way of saying the same thing. We could say that ice, water and steam represent different phases of a collection of a very large number of water molecules. Do I hear you protest that this statement is no clearer than the earlier one ? Perhaps, but there is merit in putting things this way, for we can now ask the general question: What kind of phase changes are possible when we have a large assembly of atoms or molecules ? In trying to answer this question, we discover that besides the solid ⇔ liquid ⇔ gas transitions, there are many others possible, some with rather fascinating characteristics. Indeed, once we begin thinking along these lines, we might

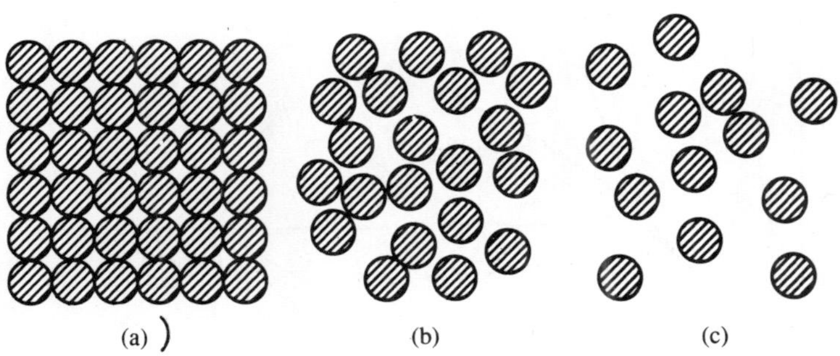

Fig.1.1 In a solid, the atoms are neatly arranged in a lattice as shown schematically in (a). When the solid melts, the order is destroyed and the packing is somewhat random as in (b). In a gas, the atoms are rather far apart as in (c) and quite free to move.

even wander off to exotic questions like: 'What happened in the early Universe? What happens inside neutron stars?' and so on! So, when we talk about the various phases of condensed matter, we are not being fuzzy. Rather, we are trying to generalise, so that we can look at many things. This is in fact what physicists enjoy most. They start with a problem and quickly widen their view so that they can take in many things. They then start a trimming operation by focussing on the central facts and throwing away all the murky details. After this, they go to work on the core of the problem. We shall see how all this works out in the case of phase change — then you will begin to appreciate the power of this approach.

Box 1.1 Suppose there is a microscope through which we can see atoms. There are graduations in the eyepiece. We adjust the microscope and note that a particular atom is at the origin at some time which we call $t = 0$ (see a). We now observe the position of the same atom t seconds later and read out the coordinates to a friend who notes them down. We repeat this experiment a large number (N) of times. We then plot on a graph paper the positions $r_1(t)$, $r_2(t)$, $r_3(t)$, ... , $r_N(t)$ obtained in the N tries (see b). Next we calculate the mean-square displacement $\langle r^2(t)\rangle$ given by

$$<r^2(t)> = \{r_1^2(t) + r_2^2(t) + ... + r_N^2(t)\}/N$$

The experiment is then repeated for various values of t, and a graph of $<r^2(t)>$ versus t is plotted. The curves we obtain (see c) would be very different for a solid, a liquid and a gas. What conclusions would you draw?

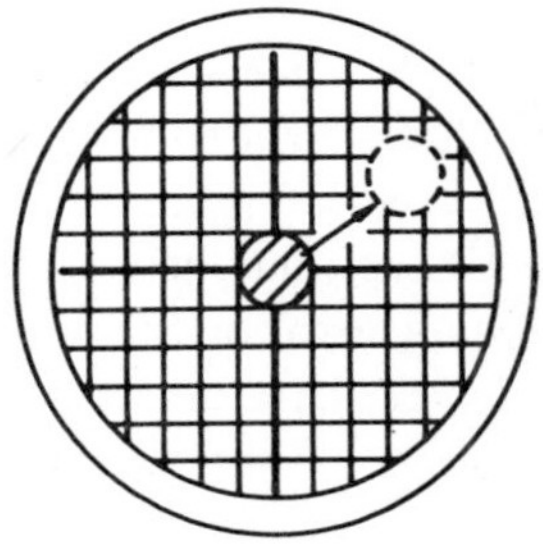

(a)

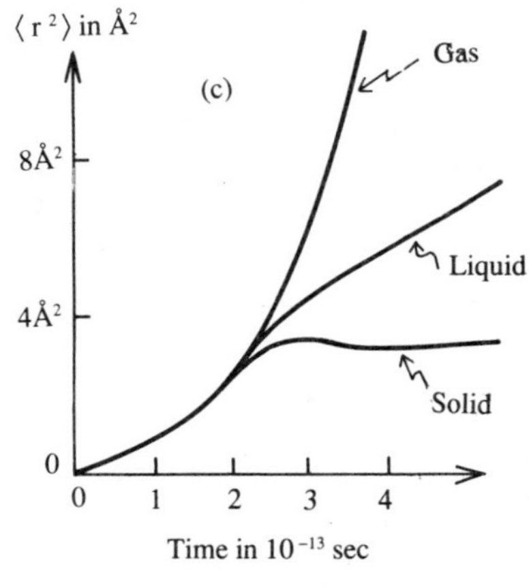

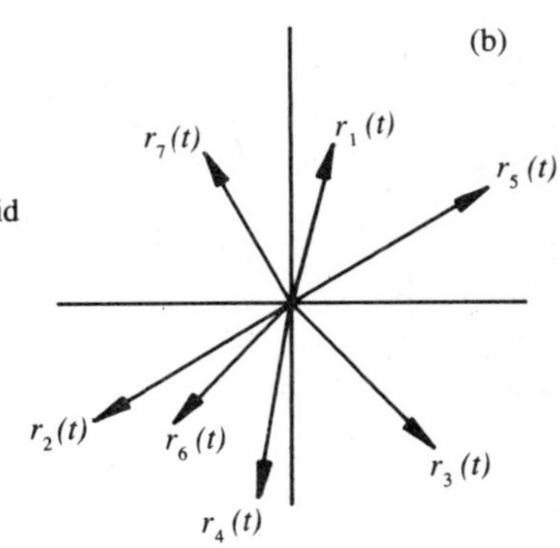

You are probably perplexed, thinking, 'What is this "phase" you are talking about ? I don't understand a thing!' Right, I admit I must define a phase for you.

A *phase* can be described as a state of matter in (thermodynamic) equilibrium. I could have given a more precise definition to satisfy the Pundits, but that would probably make you scream! Moreover, it would take the fun away. Precision *is* important, but it can wait. Now even though we want to avoid complications, we cannot at the same time afford to be too vague. I must therefore specify that the 'equilibrium' in the definition is with respect to the (thermodynamic) forces acting on the system. See Fig.1.2 and also take a minute off to study Box 1.2 which tells you some simple things about equilibrium.

Having done a crash course in equilibrium, we must next consider the kind of forces with respect to which one can talk about an equilibrium phase. Sometimes, one or more of these forces are varied while performing an experiment. They are then referred to as *control parameter(s)*. I shall use this jargon again in Chapter 6.

Let me now give you an example which will make this concept of equilibrium slightly clearer. You must have learnt the law

$$\frac{PV}{T} = \text{constant} \tag{1.1}$$

where P denotes the pressure, V the volume and T the (absolute) temperature of

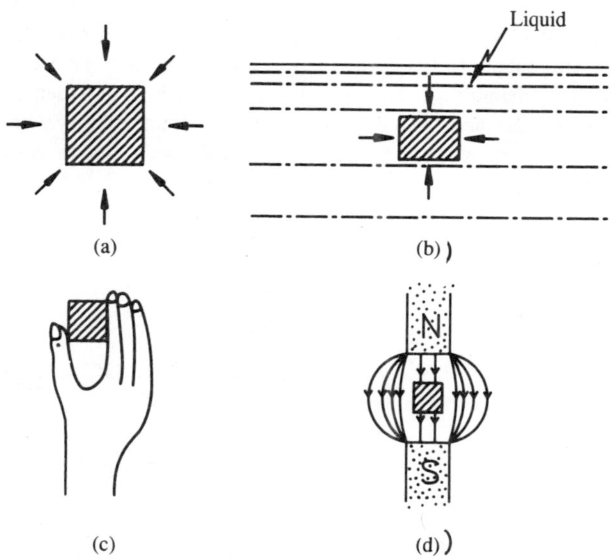

Fig.1.2 Some examples of external forces which can be applied. In (a) it is a hydrostatic pressure. The simplest way of applying this is to immerse the object in a liquid as in (b). In (c) an external stress is applied, and in (d) a magnetic field.

a certain quantity of an ideal gas. Actually, this relation holds only under equilibrium conditions. Another way of saying this is that I can make the gas have any pressure, temperature and volume I want, but only if eqn. (1.1) is satisfied can I claim that the gas is in equilibrium.

A convenient way of representing eqn. (1.1) is by the surface shown in Fig. 1.3(b). Every combination of P,V and T which satisfies eqn. (1.1) corresponds to a point on this surface. When we perform an experiment to verify this equation, we are actually recreating this surface. Note, we don't always have to be on this surface. Suppose we fire a cracker. What happens then is that first the gunpowder inside the cracker burns very quickly and produces suddenly, some gas. This gas is at a high temperature and pressure but its volume is small since it is confined by the wrapper which is still intact and has not yet come apart. The gas is then in a state *far* from equilibrium, represented, say, by a point like A in Fig. 1.3(b). It then tries to approach equilibrium, a process which is shown in

Box 1.2 The concept of equilibrium is best understood by considering the following example from mechanics. Let a bowl have a cross-section as in (a). If we gently place a marble at O and take our hands off, the marble will continue to remain there. If we try the same experiment at A, the marble will roll down to O. Position O is an example of *stable* equilibrium. Position B in (b) represents *unstable* equilibrium. No doubt the marble can be delicately balanced but the slightest disturbance will make it roll down. Position A on the wall is a *nonequilibrium* state. In general, to find out if a state q_0 of a system represents stable equilibrium, one changes q_0 to $q = q_0 + \Delta q$, where Δq represents a small displacement, and lets the system go. The state of the system will vary with time. If it approaches q_0, as shown in (c) for all arbitrary small displacements Δq, then q_0 is a state of stable equilibrium.

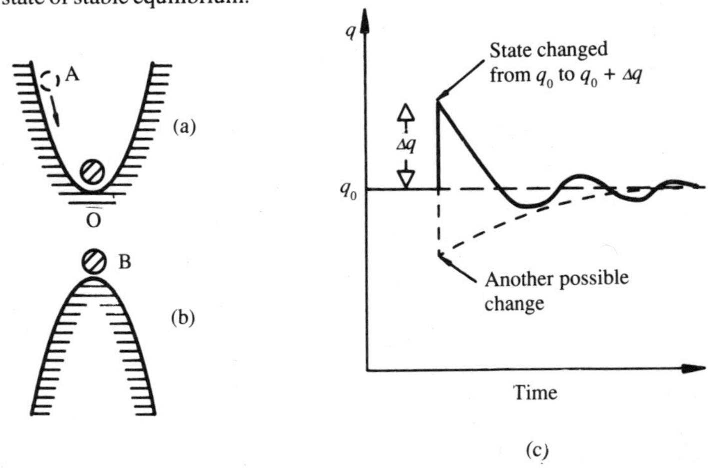

(c)

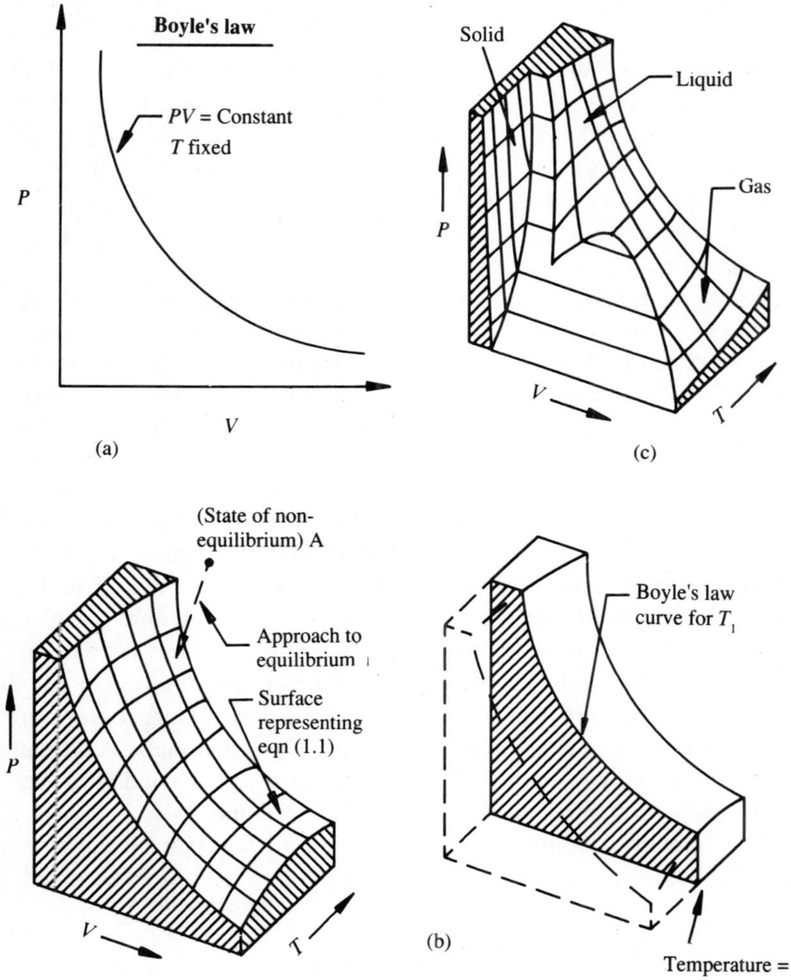

Fig.1.3 (a) Graph for Boyle's law. To represent eqn. (1.1), we need a surface as in (b). We can get the Boyle's law curve by slicing as shown on the right. If we change the quantity of gas, we change the constant in eqn. (1.1) and we will get another surface parallel to the one in (b). Points on the surface represent equilibrium states while a point like A does not. The dotted line shows a typical approach to equilibrium. When the liquid and the solid phases are also taken into account, the surface becomes as in (c).

the figure by a dotted line. It is this rapid approach to equilibrium which causes the wrapper to tear and fly apart.

Figure 1.3(b) is very simplistic because it does not represent the condensation of a gas into a liquid and the freezing of a liquid into a solid. If we consider these complications, the "mountain slope" acquires an interesting structure as in Fig 1.3 (c). We shall not go into that here but get on with our story.

Let us now ask: 'Why does a phase change occur?' You might say, 'But you have already explained that in terms of atomic motions'. True, but let me put it this way: 'How does a solid know when to melt?' Can we answer this question so that it applies not only to melting, but also to boiling and to every other kind of phase change? Well, there is an old- fashioned way of doing this; it is not quite the way in which we shall be looking at the problem later, but let's quickly see what traditional wisdom has to say.

To understand phase changes, we must consider a quantity called the *free energy*. In thermodynamics, this is perhaps *the* central quantity, and it keeps coming up repeatedly. For our purposes, a somewhat loose description of free energy will do. It is simply the sum of various energies associated with a collection of a large number of molecules or atoms. When I say large, I mean as many as $\sim 10^{22}$ or 10^{23}, because that is roughly the number of atoms which one would find in 1 cm^3 of a typical solid or liquid. In this large collection, the atoms are constantly moving, so we first have to take into account their kinetic energies. Then of course the atoms will interact with each other (see Box 1.3) and so we have to add all the potential energies of interaction. Then there are the various energies associated with the thermodynamic forces mentioned earlier. We have to keep track of them too. Depending on the circumstances, different contributions become important so that, in fact, we need different kinds of free energies to deal with different situations ! Two commonly used ones are the *Helmholtz free energy* and the *Gibbs free energy*, named after the scientists who first introduced them (see Boxes 1.4 and 1.5).

So we have this free energy. What do we do with it? Figure 1.4 gives us the answer. Shown here are the free energy curves for a solid, liquid and

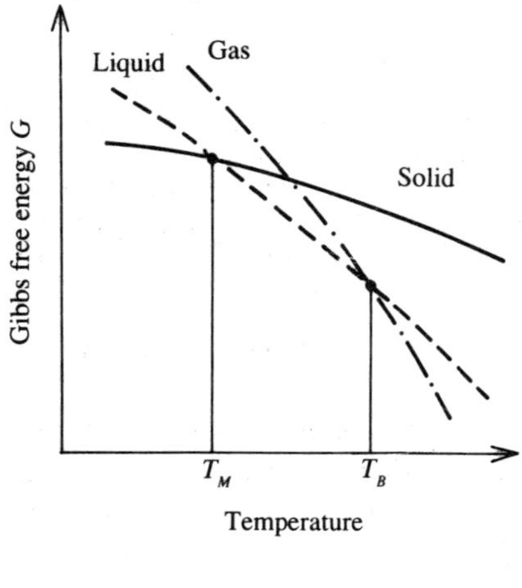

Fig.1.4 Schematic free energy curves for a solid, liquid and gas as a function of temperature. (We assume that pressure is constant, say, 1 atmosphere.) At all temperatures, Nature chooses that phase for which G is the lowest at that temperature. From this figure we can understand why the system is a solid below the melting temperature T_M, why it is a liquid between T_M and T_B, and why it is a gas above the boiling point T_B .

Box 1.3 Let's discuss here the energies relating to the interaction between particles, i.e. interaction energies. The corresponding force is easily obtained: force $= -d$ (energy)$/dr$.

Let me start with gravitation; it is said to be an attractive potential, and is shown in (a). Next we consider electrostatic interaction; it can be either attractive or repulsive, depending on the signs of the two charges q_1 and q_2. Atoms too can attract or repel each other. Interatomic forces are a bit complicated, but arise basically due to the interaction between the electrons in the outer shells of the atoms (see e). A plot of $V(r)$, the interatomic potential, looks like the graph in (c). If one atom is kept at the origin and the other is kept at some distance r which is large, $V(r)$ will be very small. As the second atom is brought close to the origin, the two atoms begin to experience an attraction which is maximum at A. At position B, the two atoms are 'in contact', and thereafter one atom tries to 'penetrate' into the other. This makes the potential repulsive.

Physicists often pretend that atoms behave like billiard balls, i.e. infinite repulsion when in contact and no interaction when the contact is broken. Such a *hard-sphere* potential is shown in (d).

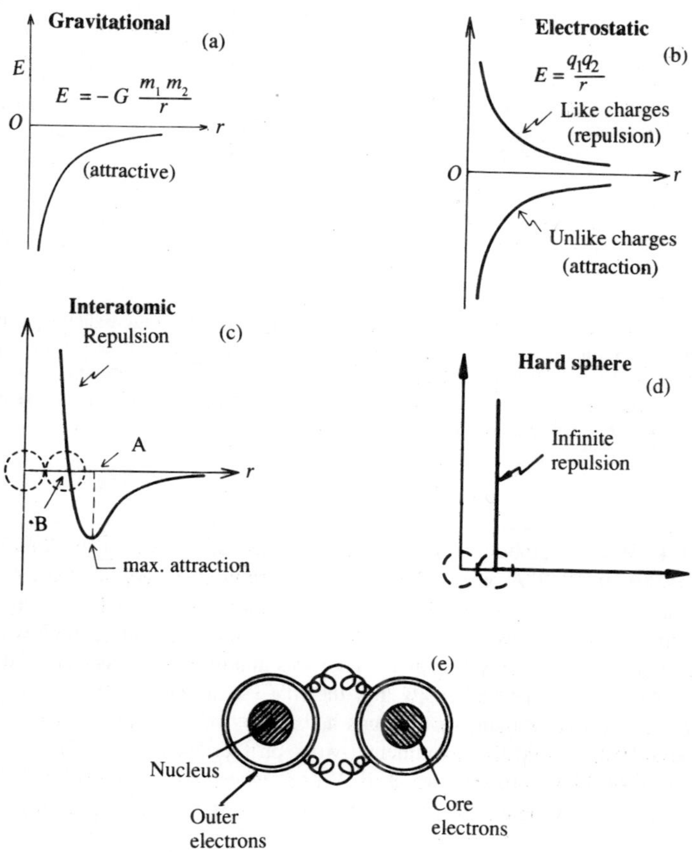

gas, as a function of temperature. The rule is that Nature will always choose that phase (as the equilibrium phase) for which the free energy is the lowest. Let us start from zero temperature (absolute zero, mind you!). Gradually increase the temperature till the melting temperature T_M is reached; throughout this range, the solid wins. Between T_M and T_B, the liquid state holds sway but beyond the boiling point T_B, the gaseous state rules supreme. It is as if Nature goes shopping and buys at the lowest price (Fig.1.5).

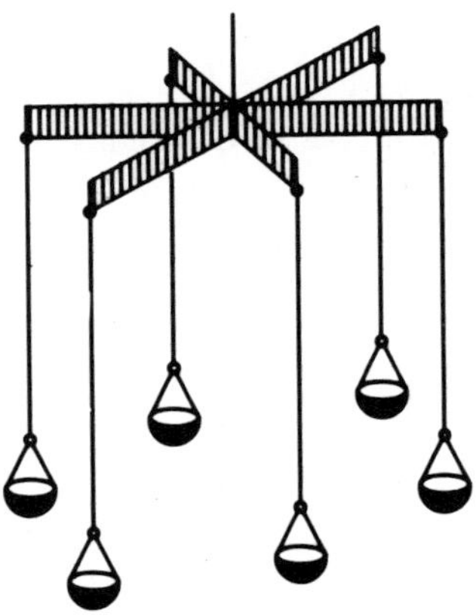

Fig.1.5 A phase transition is the result of many competing forces. This figure showing a multi-pan balance is a reminder of that. Unlike in an ordinary balance, tilting can occur here in many different ways, depending on the loads in the various pans. Likewise, a physical system can exhibit many phases. Which particular one is actually realised under a given set of conditions depends on the forces which dominate under these conditions.

Box 1.4 Willard Gibbs is one of the great physicists produced by America. He was born in 1839. A very bright student, he took up the study of engineering early on; in fact, he was the first person in America to get a Ph.D. degree in engineering. This was in 1863. He then spent a few years in Europe where his interests shifted to physics. In 1871 he was appointed Professor of Mathematical Physics at Yale University. For the first 9 years he received no salary but this was not a problem since Gibbs had money of his own. It was during this period that he did his monumental work on thermodynamics. He died in 1903. One of Gibbs' students was E.B. Wilson whose son K. Wilson we shall meet in a later Chapter. In Fig.1.4, we consider the Gibbs free energy G.

Box 1.5 Hermann von Helmholtz was born in 1821 in Germany. His father was a teacher of philosophy who taught him Latin, Greek, Hebrew, French, English, Italian and Arabic. In 1838 he entered the army medical school and graduated in 1843. One of the conditions for admission was that graduates would serve the German army for some years. Helmholtz stayed in army barracks for 8 years during which period his research continued. In 1855 he was appointed Professor of Anatomy in the University of Bonn. Helmholtz's lectures on anatomy were unusual. If he lectured on the ear, he would concentrate on the physics of the ear; if the topic was the heart, he would analyse the heart as a pump and so on. Complaints were made to the Minister, and in disgust, he went to Heidelberg in 1858 where his interests shifted completely from physiology to physics. In 1871 he became a Professor of Physics in Berlin. He died in 1894. One of the pillars of classical physics, he was C.V. Raman's childhood hero. Many of Raman's studies (including on the violin) were influenced by Helmholtz's earlier work which he had read as a young boy.

To sum up:

- We have been trying to understand what a phase is and when a phase change occurs.
- A phase is a state of condensed matter. An equilibrium phase is a phase in equilibrium under the influence of various thermodynamic forces acting on it.
- For a given system of atoms or molecules one could visualise many phases, each with its own free energy under any given conditions of temperature, pressure, etc.
- However, there is a competition between the various phases, and Nature always chooses as the equilibrium phase, that which has the lowest free energy for the conditions specified.

2 *Variety In Phases*

Phase transitions are not restricted to the solid ↔ liquid ↔ gas types discussed in Chapter 1. Many other types of changes are also possible, and almost invariably they arise on account of the complicated interaction between atoms. Surprising though it might seem, transitions are possible within the solid state itself. 'This is crazy', you might protest. But is it? Should we think of a solid merely as a lump of matter? What about the atoms inside? Probably you have caught on! Anyway, let me give a spectacular example.

2.1 Graphite and diamond

You must have heard of graphite. It is the stuff they put in pencils to make them write. (For some curious reason, we refer to them as lead pencils!) Graphite is also used in batteries, for striking arcs and even as a (solid) lubricant!

Graphite consists of carbon atoms, and is therefore the solid phase of carbon. But it is not the only solid phase for, believe it or not, diamond also is! No two materials could be so dissimilar. Graphite is black, soft and dirties the fingers. Diamond is clear, brilliant and hard. In fact, it is the hardest substance known. And yet both contain nothing but carbon atoms. Isn't that remarkable? Naturally, the interatomic forces have something to do with all this, as is explained in Box 2.1.

If graphite and diamond both contain carbon atoms, can we convert graphite into diamond? Sure we can. Not only is this a more sensible thing to try than alchemy (on which ancients wasted a lot of time) but also more interesting for Nature has already done it. How else do you think the great diamonds of the world were made?

Suppose we want to try the same experiment in the lab. How should we go about it? First, have a look at the phase diagram for carbon. A phase diagram is like a map (Fig.2.1), except that instead of the N–S and E–W directions, we have a pressure 'direction' and a temperature 'direction' (of course, axis is a better word). Pressure is nowadays measured in units of Pascal (named after the French scientist Pascal). Atmospheric pressure, also called a bar, is equal to 10^5 Pascal. High pressures are measured

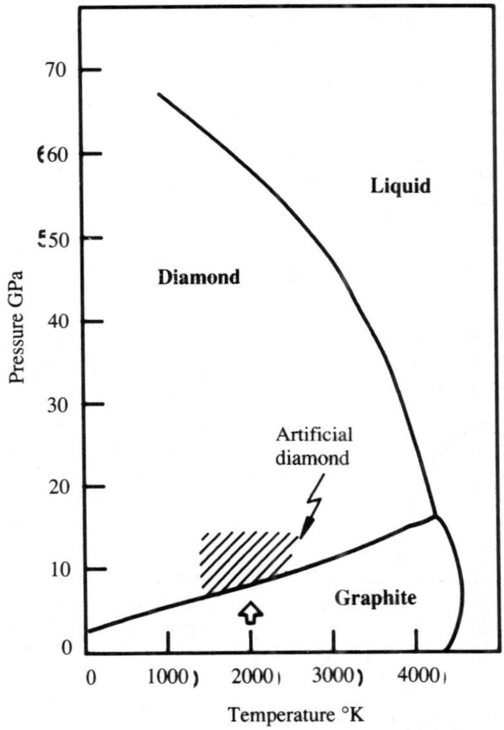

Fig.2.1 Phase diagram of carbon. The hatched area shows the region of the phase diagram where one operates to produce diamonds. The thick arrow shows how one crosses a phase boundary. Note that even though pressure and temperature are applied to convert graphite into diamond, once the latter is formed the pressure is released and the temperature is reduced. Luckily, diamond does not get reconverted into graphite. This is because it is metastable. Phase diagrams are sometimes determined by calculation, or alternately, experiments can be conducted to establish them.

in Mega (10^6) and Giga (10^9) Pascals. Old timers are more comfortable with kilobars (10^3 bars) and megabars (10^6 bars). From the phase diagram we see that if graphite is heated and simultaneously subjected to pressure (~1500 °K and ~7 GPascal), it can be converted into diamond. The diamonds so produced are small and not of gem quality. However,they are good for use as abrasives. Small, very high-quality diamond crystals have also been grown from molten carbon. This is like freezing water to make ice. But the process is very expensive and so is seldom used. For gem quality, we still depend on Nature!

How does Nature do it? Figure 2.2 gives a partial answer. Incidentally, application of pressure produces many interesting phase transitions. Box 2.2 tells you how very high pressures are generated. Besides physicists, geologists also conduct high pressure studies as it helps them figure out what is going on below the earth's surface.

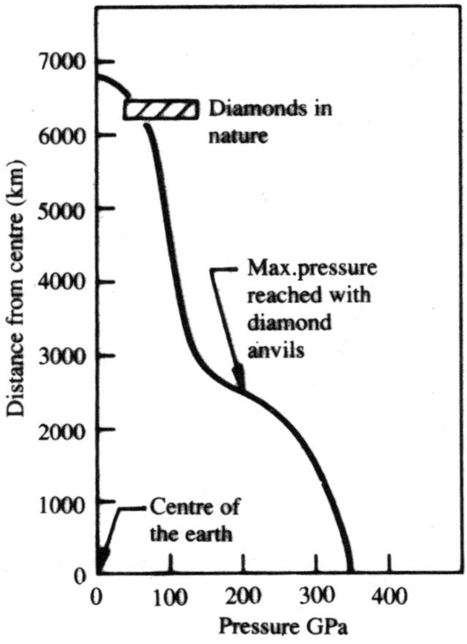

Fig.2.2 Variation of pressure with depth inside the earth. As we go down the temperature also increases. In some regions where the pressure and the temperature were both in the correct range, the carbon derived from buried organic matter got converted into diamond millions of years ago. The highest pressure reached at present in the laboratory is equivalent to going down to a depth of about 4000 km.

2.2 Metastable states

If you have been alert, you would have noticed that I have cheated a bit! I said that diamond can be made in the lab by taking graphite, heating it and applying pressure. This is what we expect from the phase diagram, and it is indeed true. After the diamond is formed, we release the pressure and allow it to cool. According to the phase diagram, if the temperature and pressure are lowered, diamond must revert back to graphite. Luckily, this does not happen! Why?

This is because diamond is in a *metastable* state. Figure 2.3 tells us what this means. Let us suppose there are two valleys as shown. We have a

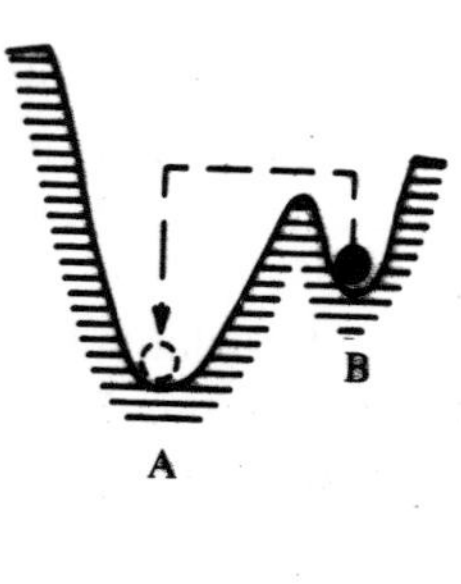

Fig.2.3 Illustration of the idea of metastability. Both A and B are minima but A is lower; it is therefore the absolute minimum. If the system is in B, it is in a metastable state. It might look like the system is in equilibrium, but if one waits long enough the system can undergo a 'thermal fluctuation'. This is the equivalent of giving a kick to the marble, making it climb the hill and roll down to the stable state. In the case of diamond, one has to wait millions of years for such a fluctuation to occur to convert diamond into graphite.

Box 2.1 The carbon atom has 6 electrons, 2 in the inner shell, and 4 in the next shell (which has a capacity of 8). In an isolated atom, these 4 electrons form a spherical cloud but, when there are neighbouring atoms to gossip with, these 4 electrons reorganise themselves. A chemist would be shocked by this language! He would instead say that the electrons reorganise into *hybrid orbitals*, and use terms like sp^2, sp^3, etc. to describe them (see b). He is right of course. These hybrid orbitals link with the corresponding ones of the neighbouring atoms to give shape to molecules as shown in (c). The pictures in (d) and (e) show how these two distinct types of orbitals lead to distinct phases of carbon. The layers of graphite atoms easily slide with respect to each other, which is why graphite acts as a lubricant.

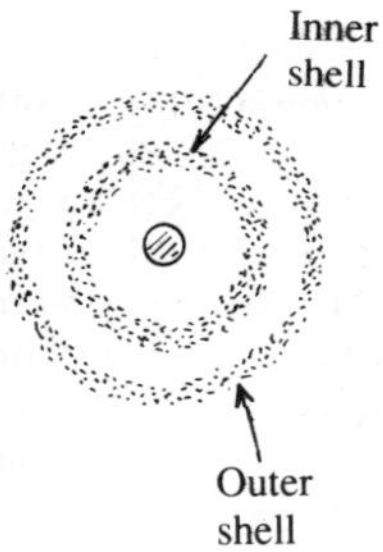

(a)

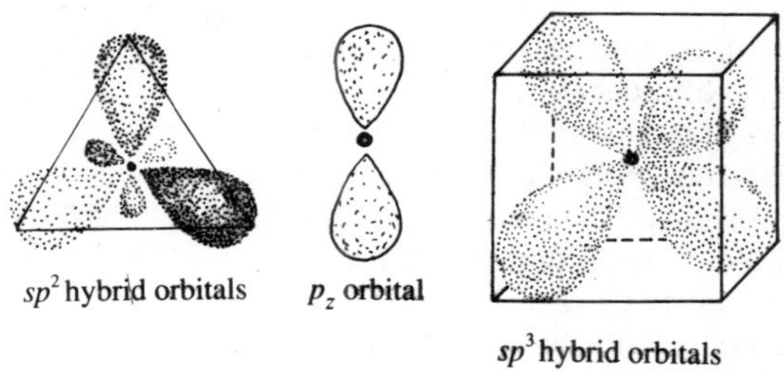

(b)

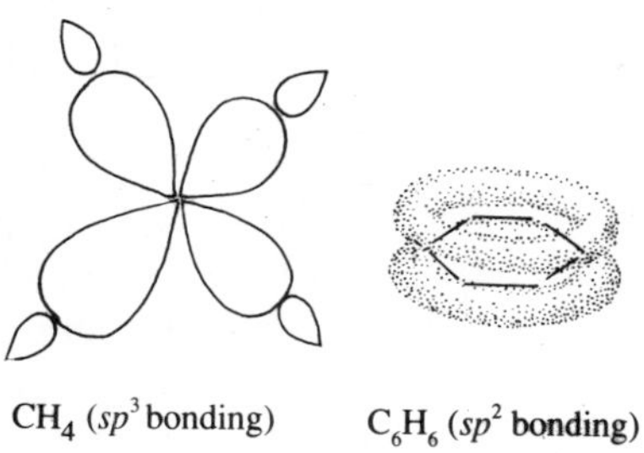

(c)

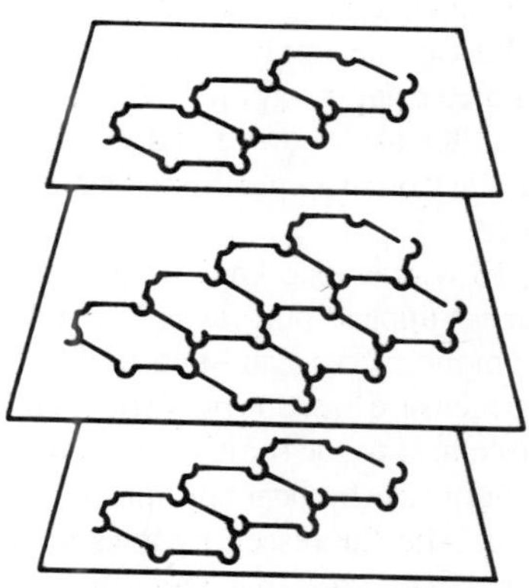

Graphite sp^2 bonding

(d)

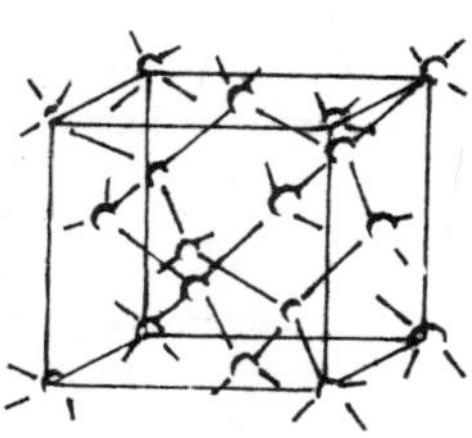

Diamond sp^3 bonding

(e)

marble at the bottom of the lower valley. We now lift it – that means we supply potential energy – climb over the hill, and place the marble in the higher valley. Once we leave it there, it will stay put there unless it is given enough energy to climb up the hill and then roll down to the lower valley.

Box 2.2 Pressure is force per unit area. To generate high pressures, one must obviously apply a large force on a small area. Of course, the material used for applying pressure should not itself crack! On account of its extreme hardness, diamond becomes the automatic choice, where affordable.

A gadget for generating very high pressures using diamond *anvils* is shown in (a). This diamond-anvil apparatus is small enough to be held in the palm of one's hand! The diamonds must be of the very best quality. The highest pressure that can be attained is shown in Fig. 2.2. The change in the structure of the solid on the applying pressure is studied using X-ray diffraction. This is rather like neutron and electron diffraction which I shall explain later.

How does one know what pressure is applied on pressing the two diamond pieces against each other? To measure this, one puts a tiny ruby piece next to the sample and makes it fluoresce by beaming ultraviolet light. The fluorescence varies with pressure, and this variation is known; therefore the pressure applied can be determined.

In India, high pressure research is being pursued among other places, at the Bhabha Atomic Research Centre, Bombay, the Indian Institute of Science, Bangalore, the Indira Gandhi Centre for Atomic Research, Kalpakkam, the National Aeronautical Laboratory, Bangalore and the Raman Research Institute, Bangalore.

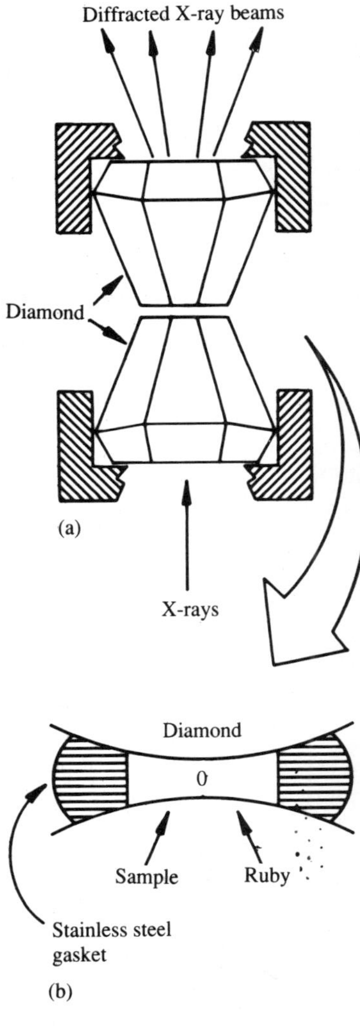

A metastable state is like the higher valley. It appears to be in equilibrium under, say, normal conditions of pressure and temperature like an equilibrium phase is, but is not the equilibrium phase because it does not have the *absolute* minimum free energy under the given conditions; this absolute minimum is in fact lower. In principle, a metastable state will be converted into a stable state if we wait long enough. That is, somehow the marble will get a kick taking it to the hill top from where it will roll down to the lower valley. A physicist would describe this as a 'thermal fluctuation'. Whether a metastable state reverts to a stable one or not depends therefore on the *probability* for such a fluctuation. Fortunately, in the case of diamond, this probability is quite low – even if we wait millions of years, it is not likely to happen! Which is good of course because that's how we can have diamonds.

By the way, diamond is not merely a gem. It has several wonderful properties. C.V.Raman was so fascinated by it, he called it the **Prince of Solids**!

2.3 Soft modes

Phase transitions are usually very sharp. For example, pure water freezes (at atmospheric pressure) at 0 °C and not at −1 °C or +0.5 °C. The question is: 'Even though the transitions themselves are sharp, are there early warning signals?' In the case of *structural phase transitions* there are (in some cases at least) early warning signals. They are called *soft modes*. By a structural transition I mean one where the crystal structure changes. The graphite to diamond change, for example, involves a change of crystal stucture.

Soft modes were discovered in 1940 by C.V.Raman and his student Nedungadi. But, even though they published their discovery in the well-known British journal *Nature*, people forgot about it. Then, roughly twenty years later, soft modes were rediscovered in Europe and in America! However, everybody is now agreed that Raman made the original discovery.

What is a soft mode? In a solid, the atoms are always moving around their equilibrium positions – fidgeting, you might say. Actually, this fidgeting motion is the superposition of various types of vibrational motions which the atoms execute in a solid. Figure 2.4 gives an example of the patterns of vibrational motions of a triatomic molecule.

A crystalline solid has an enormous number of modes of vibration – as many as $\sim 10^{23}$ modes. As the temperature is varied, the frequencies of these modes also vary. Normally, the frequency increases as the temperature is decreased but in materials undergoing a structural phase transition, one particular vibrational mode often behaves anomalously, i.e. its frequency *decreases* as sketched in Fig.2.5. In fact, its frequency

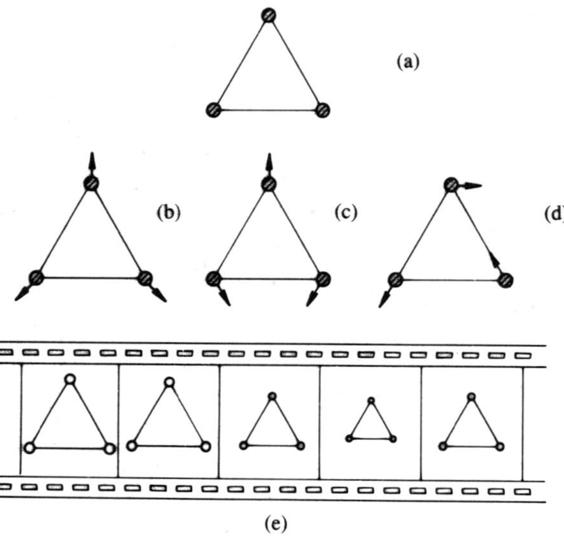

Fig. 2.4 (a) Equilibrium configuration of a triatomic molecule; (b), (c) and (d) show its different vibratory motions. That in (b) is called the breathing mode, and some of its 'motion picture frames' are shown in (e). Similar frames can be made for the other two modes.

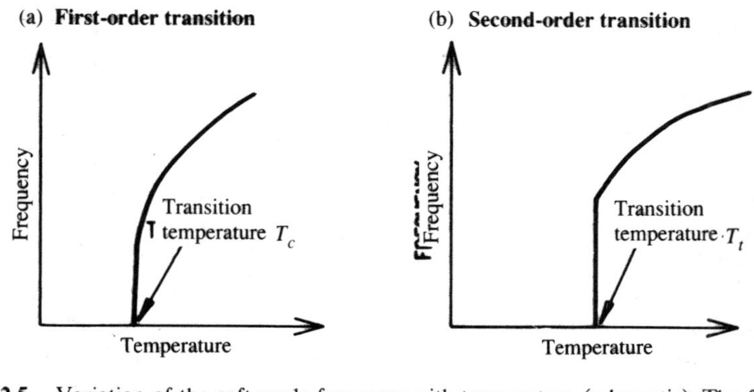

Fig.2.5 Variation of the soft-mode frequency with temperature (schematic). The frequency becomes zero at the transition temperature T_c or T_t as the case may be. In (a), the frequency approaches zero continuously while in (b) it jumps to zero suddenly. Behaviour as in (a) is seen in a second-order phase transition while that in (b) is seen in a first-order transition. The meanings of these transitions are explained in Chapter 3.

becomes zero at the transition temperature. So the two facts, i.e. the occurrence of the transition and the mode-frequency becoming zero must be connected and indeed they are. To understand this, suppose we do the following experiment. We roll a marble down the side of a parabolic bowl, as in Fig.2.6. The marble will oscillate about the bottom and, if there is no

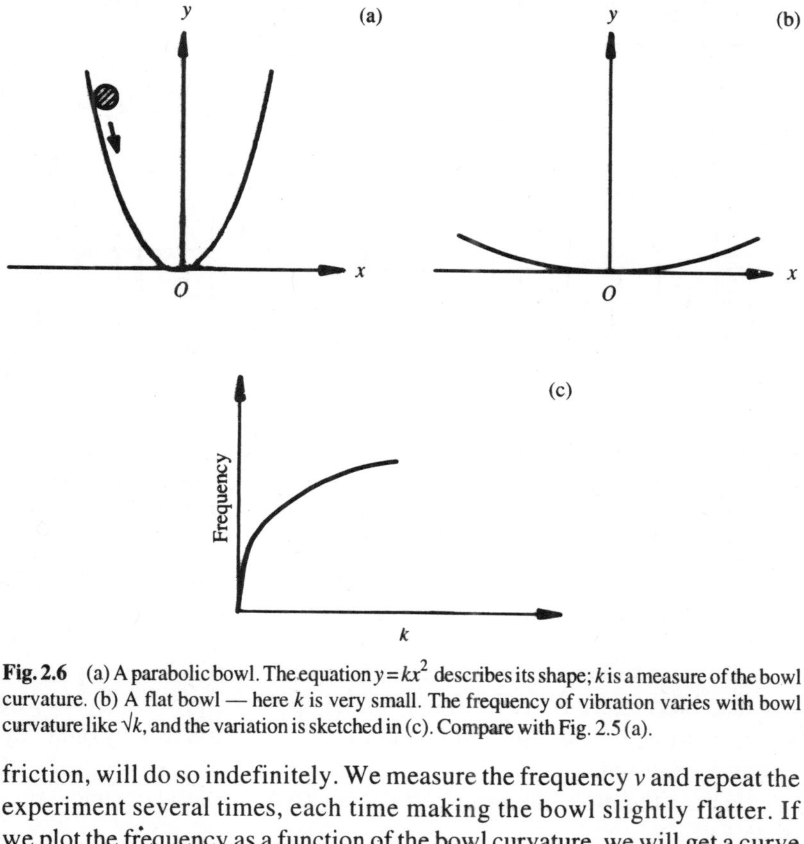

Fig. 2.6 (a) A parabolic bowl. The equation $y = kx^2$ describes its shape; k is a measure of the bowl curvature. (b) A flat bowl — here k is very small. The frequency of vibration varies with bowl curvature like $\sqrt{k}$, and the variation is sketched in (c). Compare with Fig. 2.5 (a).

friction, will do so indefinitely. We measure the frequency ν and repeat the experiment several times, each time making the bowl slightly flatter. If we plot the frequency as a function of the bowl curvature, we will get a curve as shown in Fig.2.6(c). Let us focus now on the case where the parabola is practically flat. When the marble is pushed, it does not come back because there is no force to push it backwards. The message is that when the soft mode frequency is zero, the restoring force for that mode is zero. This has far-reaching implications.

Figure 2.7 shows a square lattice of atoms. The lattice can vibrate in many ways, one of which is shown in the figure. Say this is the soft mode. When the frequency becomes zero, the lattice after getting distorted is not able to get back to its original shape. The distortion gets frozen and a structural transition is said to have taken place.

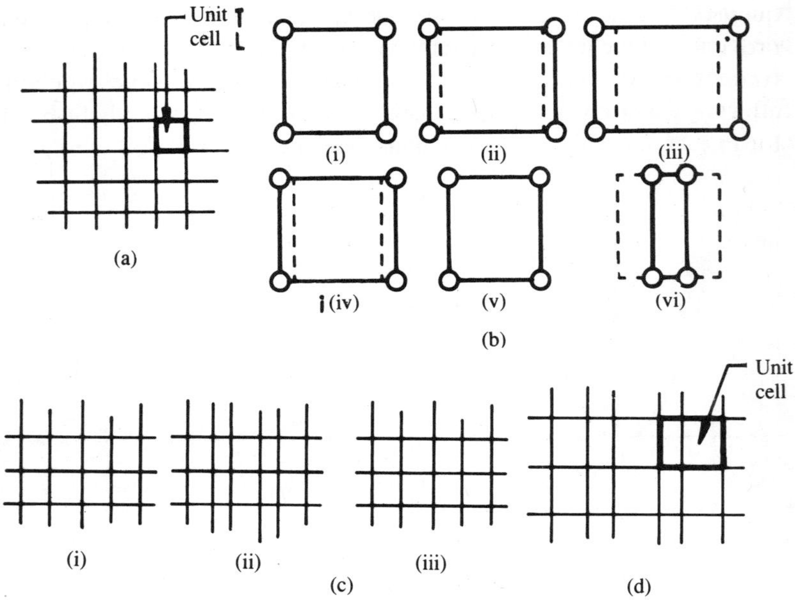

Fig.2.7 (a) A square lattice. Each cell in this lattice vibrates as shown in (b). The entire lattice then goes through a sequence of shape changes as in (c). If this is a soft mode, then the lattice can get frozen as shown in (d). Observe that the unit cell has changed from a square to a rectangle. In this process, symmetry is lowered.

2.4 Liquid crystals

Let us now move into the world of complex molecules. This is important because bio-materials are invariably made up of complex molecules. In sharp contrast to chemists and metallurgists, physicists usually fight shy of complex systems.

Consider the molecule p-azoxy-anizole (PAA) with the chemical formula

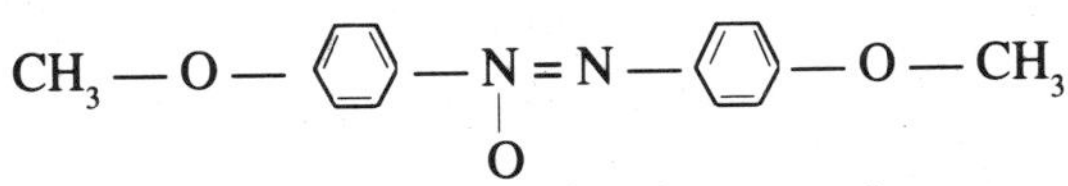

No wonder physicists avoided such substances for many years! However, physical chemists were braver – consequently, they discovered several interesting properties in such substances, besides various phase transitions. What sort of phase transitions are possible in such a substance, and how does one visualise them? The French scientist de Gennes showed the way about 25 years ago. He simply said, 'I am going to pretend that each molecule is a match stick and ask what kind of phases I can have for a bundle of match sticks?' You have here an example of the physicist's way of isolating the central fact and throwing away the rest. Once this question was posed, many things began to fall in place. One realised that order is possible not only when molecules are neatly arranged on a lattice (recall Fig.1.1a) but also when they are properly *oriented.* Orientational effects are naturally absent for atoms (since they are spherical) but not so for molecules since they are seldom spherical. In some cases like PAA, the molecules are rod-like.

Some of the arrangements possible with rod-like molecules are shown in Fig.2.8. Consider (a). We imagine the molecules to be arranged in vertical sheets stacked next to each other. In every sheet the molecules are (roughly) parallel to the vertical, but their centres are randomly positioned. Thus, as far as molecular *orientation* is concerned there is order (as in a crystal) but with respect to the *positions* there is disorder

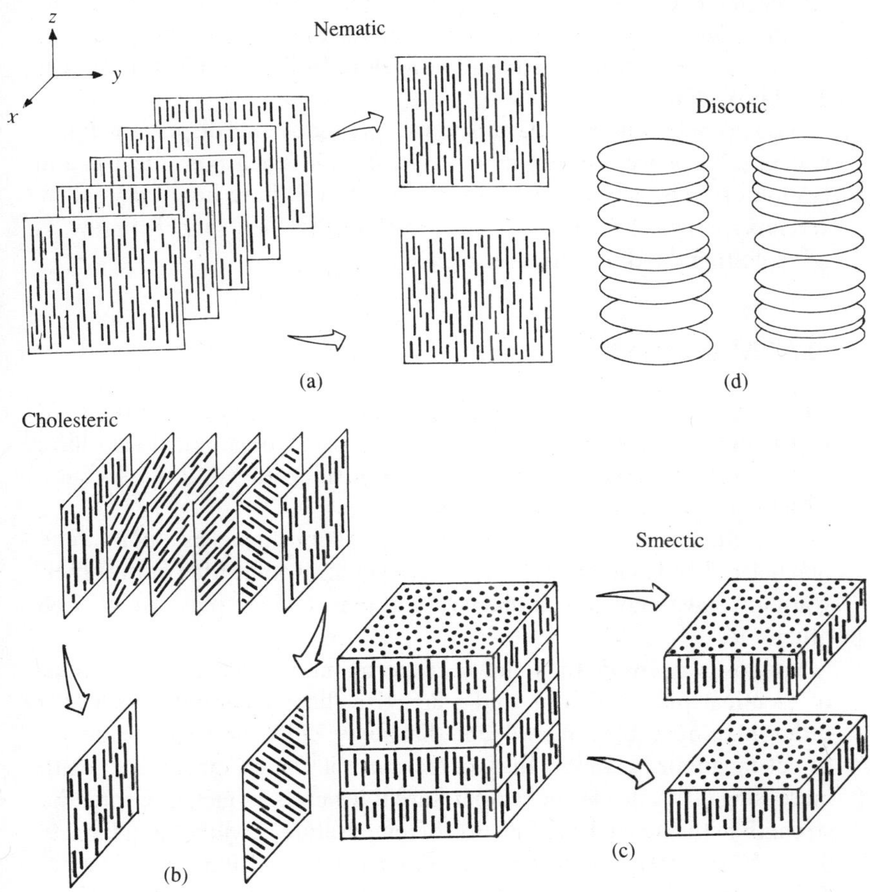

Fig.2.8 (a), (b) and (c) Various liquid crystal phases possible with rod-like molecules. The discotic phase is shown in (d).

(as in a liquid). No wonder such a phase is called a *liquid crystal* phase. In fact, this particular phase is termed *nematic*. Another kind of phase, *cholesteric*, is shown in Fig.2.8(b). Here, in any given sheet the molecules are all aligned the same way but the alignment gradually rotates from plane to plane. Naturally, if one crosses a sufficient number of planes, one comes back to the starting alignment. This distance is called the *pitch*. The phase in Fig.2.8(c) is called *smectic*. Here there are slabs neatly stacked one over the other. So in the z – direction this stacking order reminds one of a crystal. But if we look in the x – y plane and examine the 'match heads', they appear randomly distributed as in a liquid.

One does not always have to have rod-like molecules to obtain a liquid crystal phase. There are flat molecules, shaped almost like *idlis*, which can be stacked to achieve a liquid crystal phase. Such a phase called the *discotic phase* is shown in Fig.2.8(d), and was discovered a few years ago in the Raman Research Institute, Bangalore by Prof. S. Chandrasekhar and his students.

You probably know that liquid crystals are used in the displays of digital watches. They are also beginning to be used in small portable TVs and computers. The day is not far off when one will have liquid crystal TV screens as big as a wall! Engineers are clever, for they quickly find ways of exploiting the discoveries of science.

2.5 Magnetic transitions

At 770 °C, there is a phase transition in iron. It is a transition in the solid phase, but the lattice structure does not change. Iron atoms do not have rod-like or idli-like shapes. So what is the transition due to? It is associated with the magnetic properties of iron.

By itself, a piece of iron does not attract other iron pieces, but it *can* be magnetized and made to behave like a magnet. At some time or the other, you must have played with magnets and pins, making pins attract each other, etc.

Suppose we now do the following experiment. We take a large number of identical pieces of iron, and magnetize them separately, each at a different temperature. We will find that above 770 °C, iron simply refuses to get magnetized. Below that temperature it can be magnetized, with increasing efficiency as the temperature is lowered. In fact, if we plot the strength of the magnet as a function of temperature, it will be as in Fig.2.9. So 770 °C marks the transition between a magnetic and nonmagnetic state. This happens on account of the peculiar electronic structure of the iron atom. You see, the iron atom has an unfilled inner electron shell (Fig.2.10). Iron is not the only element with atoms of this type. There are

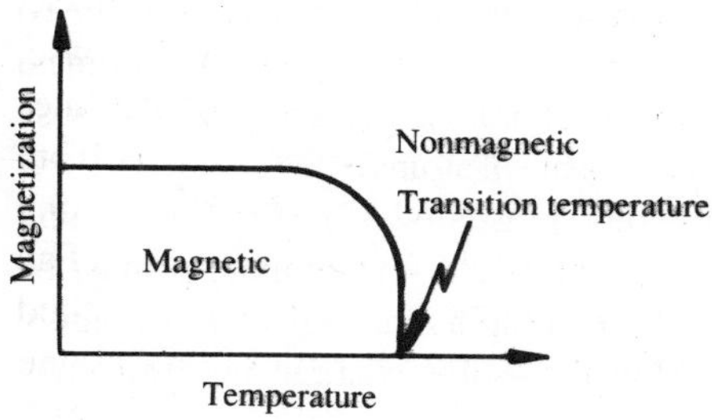

Fig.2.9 Magnetization of iron as a function of temperature (schematic).

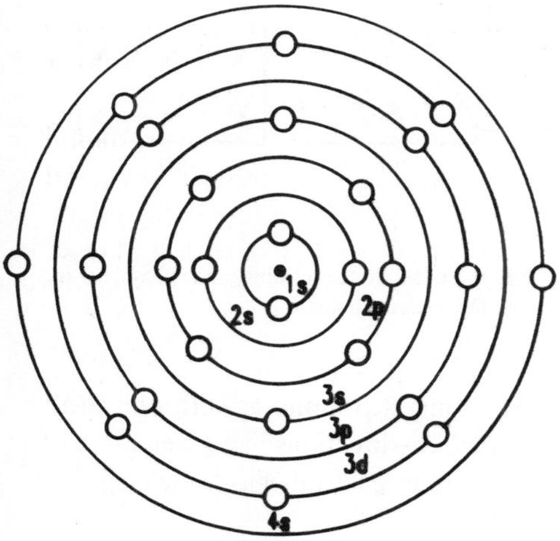

Shell	Capacity	Occupancy
1*s*	2	2
2*s*	2	2
2*p*	6	6
3*s*	2	2
3*p*	6	6
3*d*	10	6
4*s*	2	2

Fig.2.10 Arrangement of electrons in an atom of iron. The shells are labelled as is customary. Normally, the electron distribution follows the principle that the inner shells must first be completely filled before one starts filling the outer shells. On this basis, one would pack 10 electrons in the 3*d* shell. However in iron, Nature jumps to the outer 4*s* shells even before the 3*d* is filled. So iron is said to have an incomplete inner shell.

several others, and you might find it interesting to hunt for them in the periodic table. The interesting point is that all such atoms behave like tiny bar magnets. Thus, from this point of view, a collection of iron atoms is like an assembly of tiny bar magnets – atomic magnets would be a more appropriate term. The question now is: 'What kind of phases can an assembly of atomic magnets have?' In the case of iron atoms, we can say that there are two phases, one above 770 °C where iron is not magnetic as a whole, and the other below 770 °C where it is magnetic. There is a simple way of understanding this. First we must have a convention for representing an atomic magnet. The practice is to draw a small arrow. To emphasize that we are dealing with atomic magnets, we shall (sometimes) attach the arrow to a circle. Pundits refer to atomic magnets as *spins* (because they are closely related to the angular momenta of atoms).

The two phases of iron may now be represented as in Fig.2.11(a) and (b). The differences are obvious; nevertheless, a few comments must be added. Firstly, in the ferromagnetic phase the spins can collectively point in any global direction not only as in (b) but also as, for example, in (c) and (d).

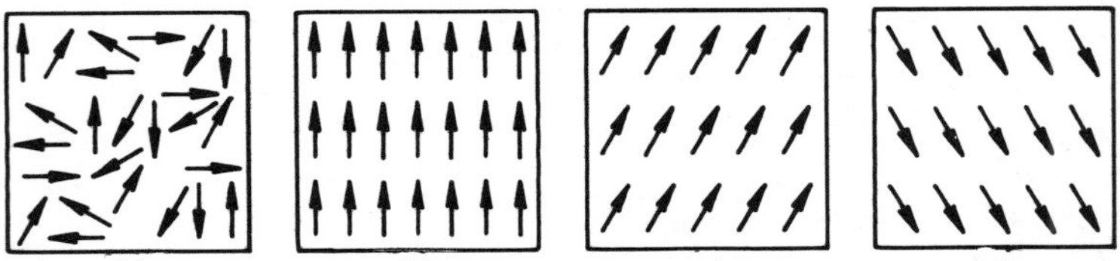

(a) (b) (c) (d)

Fig. 2.11 (a) The paramagnetic or nonmagnetic phase and (b) the ferromagnetic phase; (c) and (d) are other possibilities for spin ordering in the ferromagnetic phase.

The choice of this global direction is random. In the nonmagnetic phase (a), the *individual* spins are all pointing in random directions in a given piece of iron, cancelling each other instead of reinforcing each other as in the magnetic phase.

Incidentally, the nonmagnetic phase is called *paramagnetic*, and the phase where all the spins are aligned as *ferromagnetic*. Figure 2.11(a) is like a snapshot showing the spin orientations at one particular instant. If another photo is taken at a different time, it will show another random collection, different from the first one. This is because each spin is wildly performing its own dance! Below the transition temperature, the dancing is subdued and there is order on the average.

You might be wondering, if in a ferromagnet all spins are pointing in the same direction and reinforcing each other, then why doesn't a piece of iron behave spontaneously like a magnet? Why do we have to take the trouble of magnetizing it? This is explained in Box 2.3. You might also wonder: 'Aren't there other patterns of spin ordering?' Indeed there are, some of which are shown in Fig.2.12. Interestingly, in many substances where complex spin orderings are possible, at the very lowest temperatures there is a ferromagnetic arrangement. Is there a message in this? Think about it!

2.6 Some exotic transitions

Pressure produces some really exotic transitions. Samarium sulphide (SmS) is a good example. At room temperature and at atmospheric pressure, it has a dull-black appearance. The material is a semiconductor, i.e. its electrical conductivity is in between that of a metal (e.g. copper)

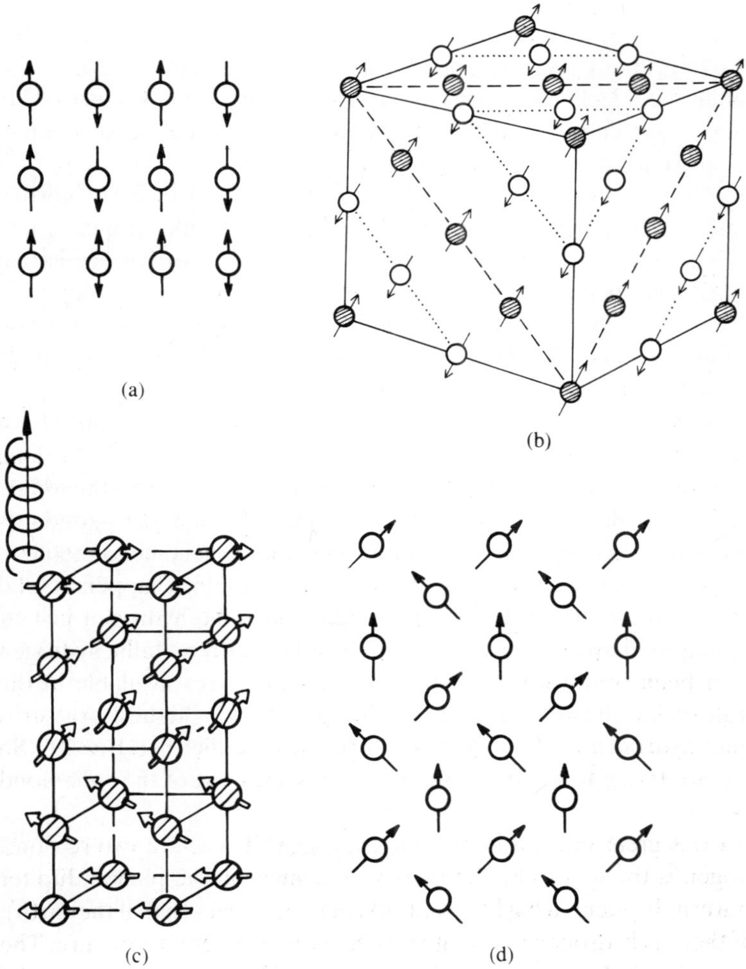

Fig.2.12 Some additional patterns of spin ordering. (a) Anti-ferromagnetic ordering. In this, the spins in adjacent layers are anti-parallel. This is shown clearly in (b). In (c) the spins in each chain spiral about a vertical axis. So this arrangement is called *helical* ordering. (d) A *canted* spin arrangement.

and an insulator (e.g. diamond). Silicon, of which transistors are made, is a well-known semiconductor.

Prof. A. Jayaraman (a student of C.V. Raman) discovered that when SmS is subjected to a pressure of about 6 kilobars, it turns from black to golden yellow in colour. In fact, Jayaraman is fond of referring to this new substance as 'fool's gold'! This yellow substance is actually a new phase of SmS. Usually, a phase change in a solid means a change of lattice structure. Not so in this high pressure transition in SmS. What happens then? Ah, something tricky and fascinating!

I shall assume that you have studied about valency in chemistry. In SmS, one expects Sm to have a valency 2^+ since S has a valency 2^-. Indeed this is true in the 'black' phase. But in the 'golden' phase, the valency of Sm fluctuates between 3^+ and 2^+. This is referred to as *valence fluctuation*, and is currently an important area of research.

Next, I would like to discuss phase transitions in iodine. At normal pressures, iodine is a solid – actually a molecular solid. It means that there is a lattice, as, for instance, in copper. But the difference is that whereas in copper each lattice site is occupied by an *atom* of copper, in solid iodine, each lattice site is occupied by a *molecule* of iodine. You probably remember that iodine is a diatomic molecule, i.e. has two atoms in it and has the formula I_2.

At normal pressures, iodine is not only a molecular solid, but also a semiconductor. Suppose that iodine is subjected to pressure. Nothing much happens till a pressure of 210 kilobars is reached, when the iodine molecules break up. The solid then becomes an honest-to-goodness atomic solid like copper. In fact, at this stage iodine becomes a metal!

Hydrogen too is a diatomic molecule. Do similar things happen in solid hydrogen? In other words, can we produce metallic hydrogen just by squeezing solid hydrogen hard enough? Until recently metallic hydrogen had not been produced even at the highest pressures available in the laboratory, but the latest advances indicate that at the highest pressures reached hydrogen is almost ready to become metallic! See Box 2.5. So people are trying to get more and more pressures out of their diamond anvils.

Why this great interest in metallic hydrogen? There are two reasons. Hydrogen is thought to be the dominant element in the planets Jupiter and Saturn. Jupiter is a big fellow (its diameter is 9 times that of the earth), and if there is hydrogen inside, it must be under very great pressure. The hydrogen inside Jupiter is probably in the metallic form, and perhaps the magnetic field of Jupiter is due to currents flowing in this metallic hydrogen.

Now for the second reason. People think that metallic hydrogen will be a superconductor at room temperature, at about 4 megabars (see Section 5.1 and Box 5.3 for information about superconductors). If that happens and if metallic hydrogen is metastable (like diamond), it opens up great possibilities. Now you should understand why physicists are chasing metallic hydrogen.

Box 2.3 In a paramagnet, the spins cancel each other (see Fig.2.11a). In a ferromagnet, the spins are supposed to be aligned, and yet a piece of iron does not behave like a magnet until it is magnetized. How is this possible? Figure (a) shows how one can have alignment and yet cancellation. There are many clusters or *domains*, and in each of them the spins are aligned. However, the domains are randomly oriented whereby there is a global cancellation. Notice that it is the clusters or domains which cancel each other and not the individual spins. Magnetization converts the multi-domain structure into a single domain as in (b).

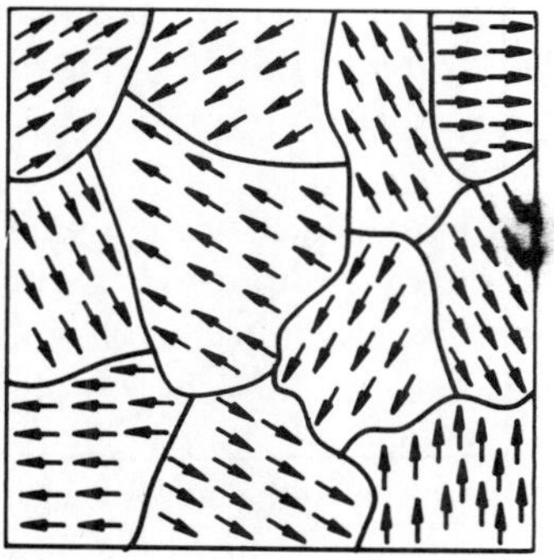

(a)

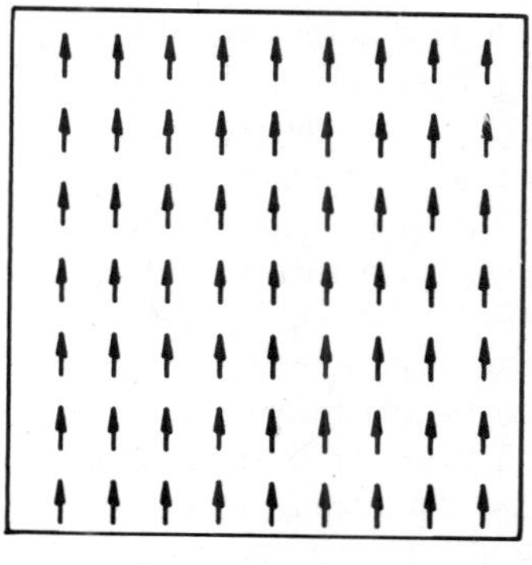

(b)

Box 2.4 How does one study patterns of magnetic ordering? The method used is called *neutron diffraction*. You know that the neutron is an elementary particle with roughly the same mass as a proton but carrying no charge. Strangely, the neutron still behaves like a tiny magnet.

Magnetic neutron diffraction consists in bouncing a beam of such magnets off an array of atomic magnets. This is of course putting things crudely! What one actually does is to start with a nice, well-collimated beam of neutrons. Such beams are available from nuclear reactors. When a neutron beam falls on a sample, the atoms in it act like obstacles and cause diffraction. Remember how the lines in a diffraction grating produce the diffraction of light? In a similar manner, the atomic array of spins causes the incoming beam of neutron spins to be diffracted. Yes, but shouldn't one have waves to obtain diffraction? Correct, but neutrons also behave like waves! Why? Try to find out!

If a system is a paramagnet, there are no sharp peaks in the diffraction pattern. With spin ordering, peaks are produced, the pattern of peaks depending on the nature of the ordering.

Neutron diffraction spectrometers operate round-the-clock at the DHRUVA reactor in Bombay. The late Dr.N.S.Satya Murthy worked actively in this area. The Indian Physics Association has instituted an award after him for young scientists.

(a)

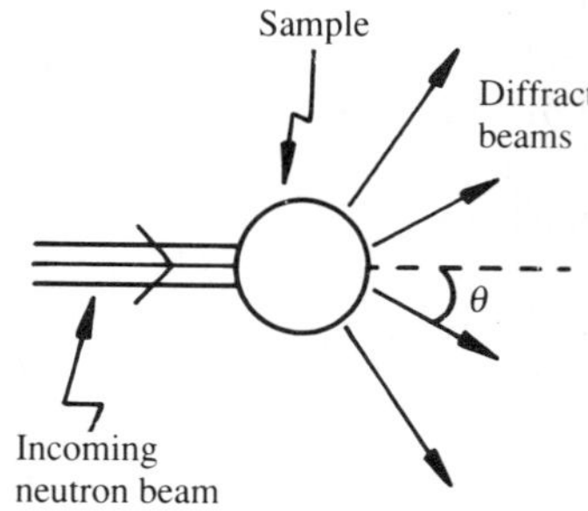

(b) **Paramagnet**

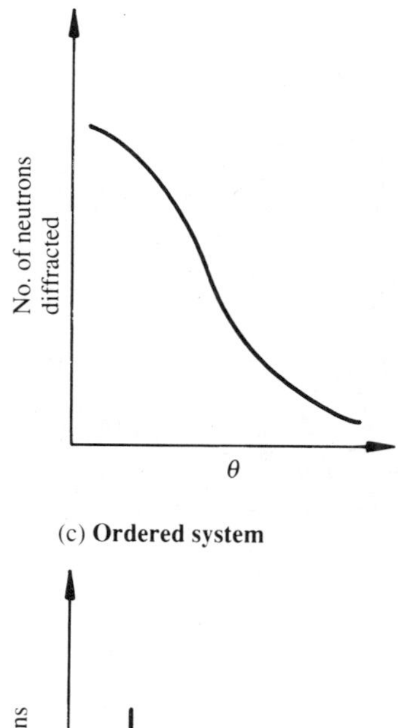

(c) **Ordered system**

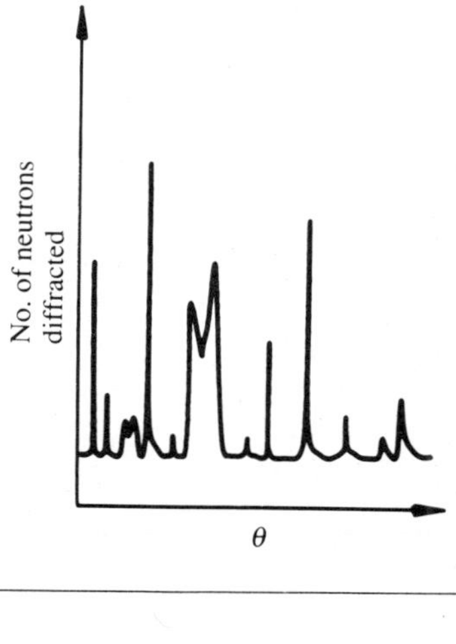

Box 2.5 Mao and Hemley of the Geophysical Laboratory, Carnegie Institution of Washington, succeeded in late 1989 in squeezing solid hydrogen to a pressure of 2.5 megabars and producing metallic molecular hydrogen — all this at room temperature. (Normally, hydrogen would have to be cooled to about 20 °K or absolute, in order for it to freeze.) At around 2 megabars, they found that a phase transition occurs. This they established by measuring the vibration frequency of the hydrogen molecule as a function of pressure — see figure. The sharp break in the vibration frequency indicates that the solid has passed from the insulating to the metallic phase. Visual examination showed that the sample had become black, confirming that a metal had been produced. However, the hydrogen was still in the molecular form. At still higher pressures the molecule is supposed to dissociate into atoms and finally, at about 4 megabars, the metal is supposed to become superconducting — at room temperature!

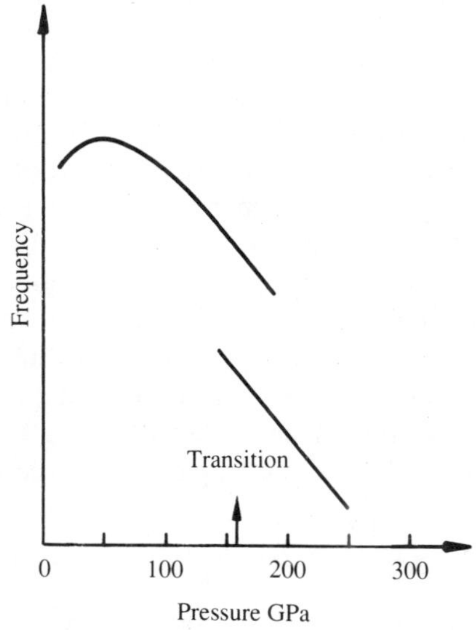

To sum up :

- There is a wide variety in the phase transitions which occur in Nature.
- Transitions are possible within the solid state itself, and can be of the structural type or magnetic, or can lead to valence fluctuations, etc.
- Systems containing molecules with non-spherical shapes show liquid crystal phases.
- Molecular solids containing diatomic molecules (e.g. I_2, O_2, N_2) all become metallic at very high pressures. And now, hydrogen does this too.

3 *Order Out Of Disorder*

You must have noticed that the transitions described so far involve a change from a disordered state to an ordered state or vice versa. We now ask: How is order born out of disorder? Notice how we generalise and focus at the same time!

3.1 Order parameter

Before answering the question just raised, we must first be able to say whether or not there is order in a system. To measure order, we use a quantity called the *order parameter*. Naturally, the order parameter must be linked to free energy because, remember, it is the free energy which will decide whether it is the ordered or the disordered state that wins.

What is the order parameter for a given phase transition? This is a tricky question, and for the moment we shall shelve it. Let me just say that in almost all known phase transitions, the order parameter has been identified. It comes in various types: as a scalar, i.e. a simple number, either positive or negative; a vector, i.e. an arrow with a length and a direction: a complex number like $ae^{i\phi}$; or something even more complicated.

3.2 Landau's theory

So we have this order parameter. What do we do with it? The brilliant Soviet scientist Landau (see Box 3.1) showed the way. Naturally his theory is named after him. We shall now consider Landau's theory in its simplest form which means that we shall suppose the order parameter is a scalar. Landau proposed that near the transition temperature T_C, the free energy of the system could be written as

$$F = a(T-T_C)\,\psi^2 + b\psi^4 \tag{3.1}$$

Here a and b are positive constants, and T is the temperature. The quantity ψ is the order parameter. Now look at Fig.3.1 which shows the graph of F versus ψ for $T > T_C$ and $T < T_C$. Nature's rule is: Always pick the state with minimum free energy. Clearly, for $T > T_C$, the

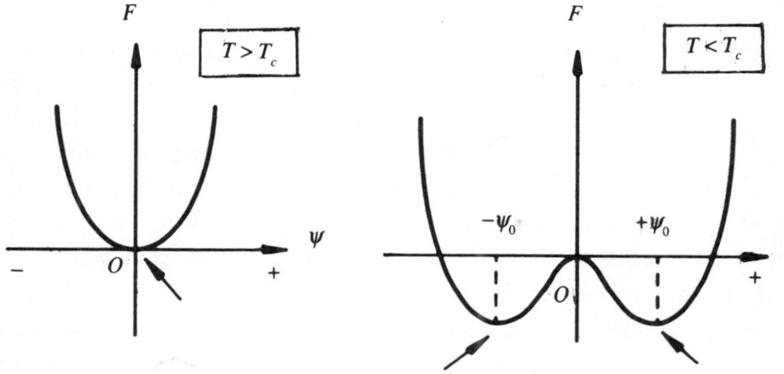

Fig.3.1 Plot of the Landau free energy function defined in eqn. (3.1) for $T>T_c$ and $T<T_c$. The slant arrows point to the minima. Observe that below T_c , the minima occur at non-zero values for the order parameter.

minimum free energy state is that with $\psi = 0$, i.e. no order; or in other words, complete disorder! Below T_c the story is different since the minimum occurs for a state with ψ not equal to zero which means that there is order. Pretty, isn't it ? Figure 3.2 says the same thing, perhaps in

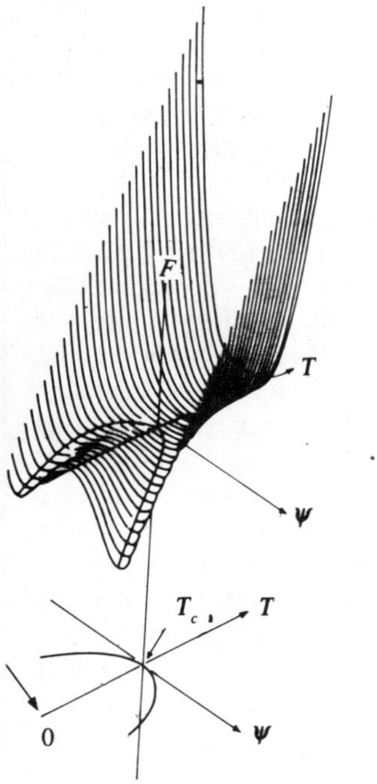

Fig.3.2 A 3-D plot of eqn. (3.1). This highlights how the free energy minima form a valley and how the valley splits (bifurcates) at T_c. The *bifurcation* is seen better at the bottom which shows the valley layout. Actually we see here how $+\psi_0$ and $-\psi_0$ vary with temperature. Caution: The zero of the temperature axis is not where you might think it is! It is shown with a small arrow at the bottom.

a slightly better fashion. We have here a whole family of free energy curves for a range of temperatures through $T = T_C$. If we place a marble on the mountain slope, it will naturally roll down to the lowest point. For $T > T_C$, the lowest point has $\psi = 0$; such points form a channel. At $T = T_C$, the main valley splits into two valleys as shown. If the marble is rolled down the main valley it will, on reaching the junction point, swing sometimes into the right valley and sometimes into the left one. The choice will be random. This is an important point, and I shall come back to it later. For the present, I would like you to note a few other things.

Firstly, what is the meaning of a state with order $+\psi_0$? A scalar order parameter applies to a case where there are spins (recall our discussion about spins in Chapter 2) which can point only up or down as shown in

Box 3.1 Landau is a great name in physics but curiously enough, most physicists would be hard put to say what he is famous for! But everyone would know about his books which are a story in themselves.

Landau was born in USSR in 1908. As a young man he had the opportunity to spend some time with Niels Bohr and to meet all the founders of quantum mechanics. He returned to the Soviet Union with all this knowledge and worked for a while in Leningrad. In 1932 he moved to Kharkov where he started a programme for his students. Meanwhile, Kapitza (see Box 5.1) returned to the Soviet Union from England, and Landau joined him in Moscow in 1937. There were terrible political problems in Russia at that time, and unfortunately Landau was taken to be an enemy of the state and thrown into prison. In fact he was about to be put to death but Kapitza intervened, and Landau was both saved and released. Landau celebrated with a series of discoveries, which included an explanation for superfluidity (see Chapter 5).

In Moscow Landau perfected his training scheme. Students were selected after a stiff entrance exam. Thereafter they went through an even stiffer training course which lasted many years. They had to learn several subjects, including hydrodynamics which students of physics were not usually taught. Later, Landau, assisted by his student Lifshitz, developed his lectures into a series of books — the famous Landau–Lifshitz series. Only about 40 students completed the course in over a decade and a half. Most of them have since become famous.

In 1962, a truck hit the car Landau was travelling in, and he was seriously injured. Medicines poured in from all over the world, and Canada flew a famous neurosurgeon to Moscow to perform brain surgery. Landau survived, but he was never again the same. It took a long time for his memory to come back. He could not do science again, but kept his spirits alive by reading poetry. He died in 1968. He will be remembered not only for his work on superfluidity (for which he received the Nobel Prize while in the hospital), but also for many other things such as his work on diamagnetism, superconductivity, damping in plasmas, Fermi liquids, and above all, for being a **complete** physicist. An Institute called the *Landau Institute for Theoretical Physics* has been established in Moscow in his honour.

Fig.3.3. In this case, +ve values of ψ imply that the majority of the spins are up while −ve values imply that the majority are pointing down. So when the spins order, there are two basic patterns to choose from, and Nature randomly picks one of these.

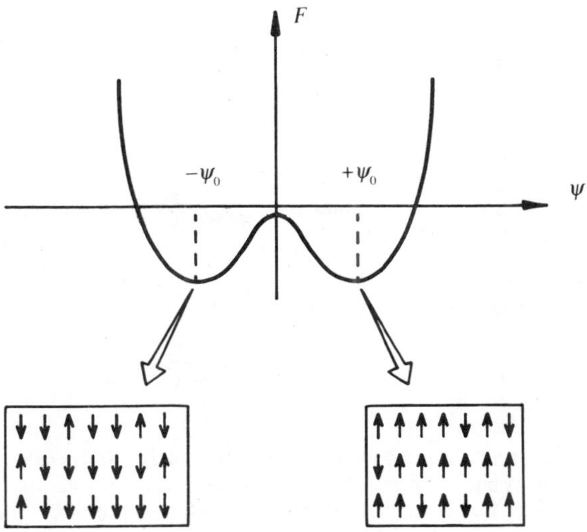

Fig.3.3 Meaning of $+\psi_0$ and $-\psi_0$ illustrated with a simple example. Here the system has spins which can point either up or down. The number of up spins minus the number of down spins equals the value of ψ_0. If this is a positive number, then it means that the up spins are in the majority. The magnitude of this number increases as the temperature is lowered, the variation being as in Fig.2.9. See also the lower part of Fig.3.2.

3.3 Symmetry and order

Choosing a state of minimum free energy is only one part of the story. There is something else, which is not only important but also fascinating. Before discussing that, we must first know something about symmetry.

Let us compare a mango tree with an equilateral triangle. No, I am not being crazy! As you will presently see, I have a point to make. A mango tree is no doubt beautiful but it is not a geometrically symmetrical object whereas an equilateral triangle is.

Can we define symmetry? Poets and artists will no doubt have their own definitions but in physics, symmetry is related to a concept called *invariance*. Let us go back to the equilateral triangle. Take a good look and close your eyes. While you are doing so, I rotate the triangle through 120°

as shown in Fig. 3.4. I now ask you to open your eyes and say whether I have done anything to the triangle. You would not be able to give a definite answer because whatever you are now looking at would be identical to what you saw earlier. Instead of a clockwise rotation through 120°, I could have performed an anticlockwise rotation through 120°, and once again you would not be able to guess that I have done something to the triangle.

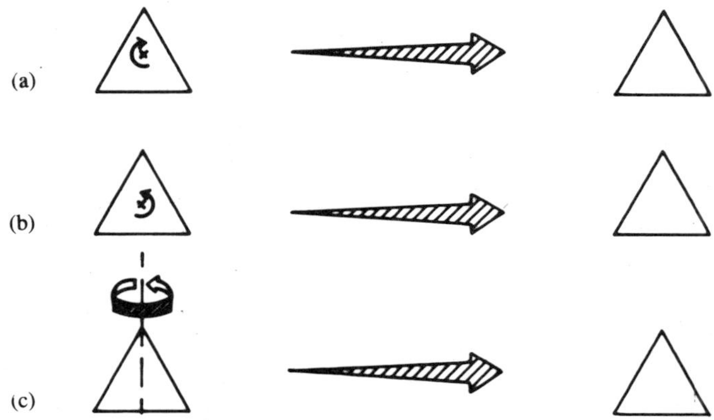

Fig.3.4 Some of the invariances of the equilateral triangle. (a) Triangle going into itself after a 120° rotation about the centroid. (b) Similar thing happening for a 120° anticlockwise rotation. (c) A 180° flip about the dashed line, which also leaves the triangle invariant.

I could also have flipped the triangle about the dashed line through 180° and so on.Thus, there are many operations I could perform which would bring the triangle back into coincidence with itself. This is invariance — things appear absolutely the same before and after. Of course, there is no invariance if I try arbitrary rotations, by 7.3° for example, but the point is that there *are* operations which leave the equilateral triangle invariant.

I must now use more respectable language and avoid colloquial terms. I will not talk about an object either. I will instead consider systems — a system of atoms or a system of spins, for example — and I would like to perform *operations* on the system. Putting it another way, I could say that I would like to subject the sysem to a *transformation*.

A transformation that leaves the system invariant is called a *symmetry transformation*. In the case of the equilateral triangle, several such transformations exist — I described a few of them. So clearly the triangle possesses some symmetry. Using the same yardstick, it is easy to see that the mango tree has no symmetry at all. A purist would object and say that the mango tree has *trivial symmetry*. What it means is that there is an operation called the *identity* operation which leaves the system, i.e. the mango tree, invariant. And what is this identity operation? Leaving the system alone, of course! You might consider the identity operation utterly silly; not quite – mathematicians are not dumb you know, and they do things with a purpose! Having the identity operation is useful for some book keeping. In some sense, this is like the role played by zero in arithmetic. By the way, in physics one deals not only with the invariances of objects or systems but also of energy, equations, physical laws, etc. We shall have an example soon.

Now that we have a way of detecting symmetry, we can also compare. Consider a circle and a square. Which has more symmetry? Simple. Just count the number of symmetry operations of the circle and of the square and see which is bigger. Clearly the circle wins. I mean you can rotate the circle by arbitrary angles θ (Fig.3.5) and the circle will go into coincidence

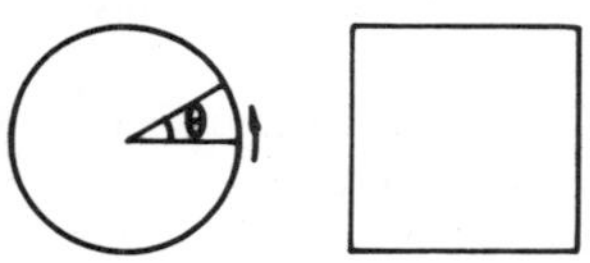

Fig.3.5 Symmetry operations of a circle and a square. A circle is invariant under rotations through arbitrary angles θ. There is an infinity of such symmetry transformations. A square has fewer symmetry transformations and therefore has less symmetry than a circle.

with itself. There is an infinity of such symmetry transformations. In the case of the square, this number is finite. (You might like to spend a few minutes to find out what this number is.)

What has symmetry got to do with phase transitions? Plenty! Let us find out. We go back to the Landau free energy in eqn(3.1) and study its invariances. F depends on ψ, and we ask: What are the things we can do to ψ which leave F invariant? Let us try changing ψ to $\psi' = (\psi + 1)$. The free energy now is

$$
\begin{aligned}
\text{New free energy} &= a(T - T_C)\,(\psi')^2 + b(\psi')^4 \\
&= a(T - T_C)\,(\psi + 1)^2 + b(\psi + 1)^4 \\
&= a(T - T_C)\,\psi^2 + b\psi^4 + \text{some stuff} \\
&= F + \text{some stuff} = F', \text{ say.}
\end{aligned}
$$

This 'some stuff' is generally not zero, and so F is different from F'. Hence the transformation $\psi \rightarrow \psi'$ is not a symmetry transformation. Is there any such symmetry transformation at all? Sure. Try changing ψ to $-\psi$. This operation is called reflection (symbol R), and it leaves F unchanged. In fact, besides the identity (E) and the reflection (R), there are no other transformations which leave F invariant. The set (E, R) is called a *group* because it has some special properties (see Box 3.2). We shall denote the above group by the symbol C_2. Observe that as far as F is concerned, it does not matter whether $T > T_c$ or $T < T_c$. It is always invariant under the group C_2.

Box 3.2 You must have heard of sets — set of animals, a set of numbers, and so forth. Let us say we have a set (E, A, B, C, D, F). This is a *finite* set consisting of six *elements*. It is possible to have operations (or compositions) between elements of a set. What this means is that if the set consists of the numbers (0, 1, 2, 3,...), then an operation between two elements could mean adding two numbers, multiplying two numbers, etc. When element A operates on B, we express it as AB. The result of the operation could be another element belonging to the set, e.g. 1 + 2 =3. We would be interested in such cases, and write the result as $AB = C$.

A *group* is a very special kind of set which has the following properties:

1. For every element (e.g. A and B) in G, the operation AB results in an element contained in G.
2. There is *associativity*, i.e. $(AB)C = A(BC)$. It means that B can first act on C, and then A can act on the result or A first acts on B and the result of that is made to act on C.
3. There is a special element E in G such that if you operate on any element with E, you get back the same element, i.e. $EA = A$, $EB = B$ and so on. This element E is called the *identity* element. We have met it before.
4. For every element A in G, there exists some other element Y say, such that $AY = YA = E$. Often, Y is written A^{-1}, and read A inverse.

Look at the table below. It is a multiplication table, and tells you what happens when one of the elements of our set acts on another, e.g. $BA = E$. Using this table, you can convince yourself that all the group properties are obeyed by our set (E, A, B, C, D, F). This abstract group has the label D_3.

Element acting first	Element acting second					
	E	*A*	*B*	*C*	*D*	*F*
E	*E*	*A*	*B*	*C*	*D*	*F*
A	*A*	*B*	*E*	*F*	*C*	*D*
B	*B*	*E*	*A*	*D*	*F*	*C*
C	*C*	*D*	*F*	*E*	*A*	*B*
D	*D*	*F*	*C*	*B*	*E*	*A*
F	*F*	*C*	*D*	*A*	*B*	*E*

You may ask, 'So what ? Is there any use ?' Yes, and to see that, consider an equilateral triangle. I have already discussed various geometrical operations which will leave the triangle invariant, i.e., bring it back into coincidence with itself. Let us now make identifications as below:

A = 120° rotation, B = 120° anticlockwise rotation, C, D, F = 180° flips about the dotted lines a,b,c in the figure, and E = identity..

We then find that the geometrical operations defined above obey the multiplication table we had before. In other words, the set of operations we can perform on an equilateral triangle is a realisation of the *abstract* group D_3 introduced earlier.

Once we know that a physical system has group structure, then using that knowledge, we can describe many of the properties of the system. For instance, using group theory, one can sketch the different modes in which the membrane of a drum can vibrate. We don't need to know anything else about the drum such as its diameter, the density of the membrane, etc. Group theory is very powerful, and there are many useful things one can do with it.

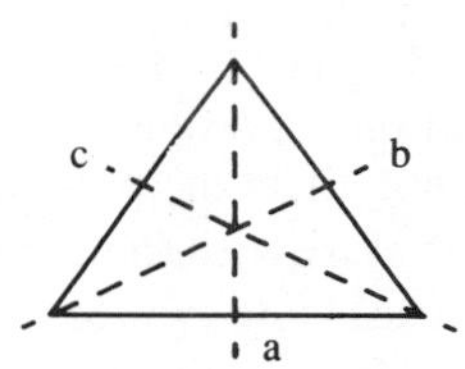

What about the state of minimum free energy? This is a different story. Let us use the symbol Ψ to denote this particular state. Of course, for $T > T_c$, Ψ has the numerical value zero. What we are interested in is the fact

$$E\Psi = \Psi, R\Psi = \Psi \tag{3.2}$$

The first of the above two results simply says that if I don't do anything to Ψ, it will remain Ψ, naturally! The second says that if I reflect Ψ, I get back Ψ. This is because Ψ in this case is zero. So, the long and short of it is that the minimum free energy state Ψ is also invariant under the group C_2 as F is. In other words, Ψ *has the same symmetry as F*.

What happens below T_c? The system orders, and has two options which we call Ψ_1 and Ψ_2 say. Of course we know from Fig. 3.1 that Ψ_1 and Ψ_2 are mirror images of each other. Let us say that the system has (randomly) chosen Ψ_1. We then have,

$$E\Psi_1 = \Psi_1 \text{ and } R\Psi_1 = \Psi_2 \tag{3.3}$$

and likewise, if Ψ_2 is chosen,

$$E\Psi_2 = \Psi_2 \text{ and } R\Psi_2 = \Psi_1 \tag{3.4}$$

Either way, the ordered state is *not* invariant under the group C_2. So we have the following picture. In the disordered phase, the thermodynamic state (this is our name for Ψ) has the same symmetry as F, whereas in the ordered phase it has less symmetry. This is a remarkable change. At T_c the *symmetry becomes less but the order becomes more*. Nature trades symmetry for order! This is referred to as symmetry breaking. In the example considered, it is reflection symmetry that is broken.

3.4 Symmetry breaking in some transitions

If symmetry breaking is really true, then, could we possibly understand the liquid ↔ solid transition in this language? Sure. I will cheat a little bit here because F for the above transition is not quite given by eqn. (3.1) but by a slightly different expression since the liquid ↔ solid transition represents what is called a first-order change. However, this does not affect the present discussion.

Let us start with the symmetry of the liquid. Would you believe that a liquid has more symmetry than a crystal? We can easily convince ourselves of this fact. Look at Fig. 3.6(a). It shows the distribution of atoms in a

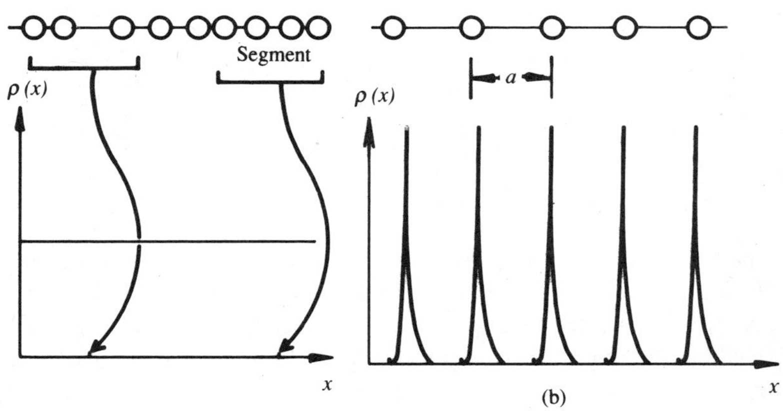

Fig.3.6 Illustrated at the top are atomic chains representing a 1-dimensional liquid (see a) and a 1-dimensional crystal (see b). Both are supposedly infinite in extent. The corresponding density distributions are shown below the chains. They are obtained by 'measuring' the density in small segments along the line. The liquid density is constant throughout, and therefore remains invariant under arbitrary translation. The density for the crystal remains invariant only under the lattice translation a and multiples of it.

1-dimensional liquid. Don't worry that liquids really exist in 3 dimensions and not in 1 dimension. I am just trying to make a point. Remember the definition of density? It is mass per unit volume. In this case we modify it to mass per unit length. We take short segments as shown in Fig. 3.6, calculate the mass for each segment, divide by the segment length and thus obtain a value for the density which we assign to the point corresponding to the centre of the segment. If we do this throughout the length of the liquid, we will obtain the *density distribution* $\rho(x)$ for the liquid. It is as if we took a 'density meter' and dragged it across the liquid, noting down the readings along the way. If we do the same thing for a crystal, we will get a different result, which is also shown in Fig.3.6. By the way, a well-known British scientist named Rudolf Peierls (of Oxford) has proved that a 1-dimensional crystal will be unstable and would undergo distortion. For the moment we shall ignore that and pretend that such a 1-dimensional crystal can exist without distortion or whatever.

OK. Let us go back and study Fig.3.6. The difference between $\rho(x)$ for the liquid and that for the crystal is striking. Let us try to 'slide' $\rho(x)$ for the liquid. We find that $\rho(x)$ does not change its appearance no matter how much we slide. In the case of the crystal, $\rho(x)$ will go into coincidence with itself only when we slide it in discrete steps. The minimum step length required for such coincidence is the *lattice spacing* a. We can also slide by multiples of a.

Let us put all this into a language that a physicist would be more comfortable with. We will say that the density function of our 1-dimensional liquid is invariant under the *continuous* group of translations $\mathfrak{J} = \{t\}$, where $\{t\}$ denotes the set of *all possible translations* along x. The density function for the crystal is invariant under the *discrete* group $T = \{t_n\}$ where $\{t_n\}$ denotes the set of translations na, n being an integer, either positive, negative or even zero. It is clear that T does not contain all the operations of $\mathfrak{J}$, but all the operations of T are contained in $\mathfrak{J}$. Therefore, T is said to be a *subgroup* of $\mathfrak{J}$. So when our 1-dimensional liquid freezes to become a 1-dimensional crystal, *it breaks continuous translational symmetry* (*in 1 dimension*).

We shouldn't really stop here because this example does not tell the full story. So we move into 2 dimensions (Fig.3.7). Now we can not only translate (i.e. in 2 dimensions), but also rotate. We can in fact translate, rotate or do both. Therefore, let us denote a general operation by the symbol $(R\,|\,\boldsymbol{t})$ where R denotes rotation and $\boldsymbol{t}$ denotes translation. We shall adopt the convention that rotation is performed first and then the translation. How do I represent pure rotation? Very simple – I just write $(R\,|\,O)$. What about pure translation? I write $(E\,|\,\boldsymbol{t})$ where E denotes the identity operation in the group of rotations; clearly then $(E\,|\,\boldsymbol{t})$ denotes translation by $\boldsymbol{t}$.

A 2-dimensional liquid (of infinite extent) is invariant under the Euclidean group $E(2) = \{(R\,|\,\boldsymbol{t})\}$ which simply means I can rotate by any amount I please and also translate in any direction by any amount I please!

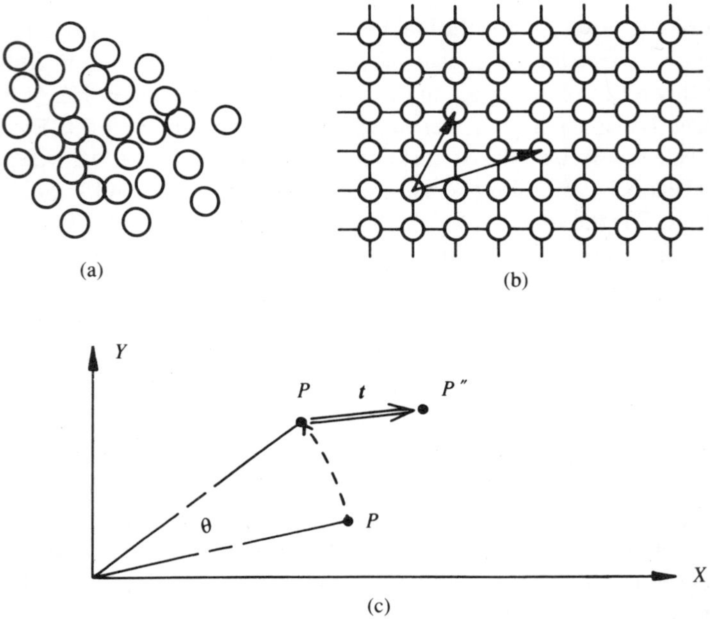

Fig.3.7 (a) A 2-D liquid and (b) a 2-D crystal; (c) illustrates the effect of the operation $(R\,|\,t)$. R makes a typical point P go to P'; the translation t then takes P' to P''. So the net effect of $(R\,|\,t)$ is to move P to P''. The arrows in (b) show typical lattice vectors t_L. By the way, both the liquid and the crystal are supposed to be infinite!

What about a crystal? Ah, here there are restrictions and not all the translations we earlier considered are allowed. Only lattice translations t_L defined by

$$t_L = n_1 a + n_2 b \quad (n_1, n_2 \ \textit{integers})$$

are allowed. Also I cannot rotate by any amount I like. Only *certain* rotations are allowed. In fact, if you think about it for a while, you will notice that the rotations which are allowed are sort of 'linked' to the permitted translations. It is as if Nature gives us the crystal with strings attached – it also presents us with a 'package deal' of allowed translations and rotations. In a nutshell, when a 2-dimensional liquid freezes, it breaks both continuous translation as well as continuous rotational symmetry.

The group of restricted rotations and translations possible in crystals is given a special name – *Space Group. Space groups are subgroups of the Euclidean group.*

By the way, independent of physicists and their interest in crystal structure, symmetry breaking and stuff like that, mathematicians had already figured out the number of possible space groups not only in 2 and 3 dimensions, but even in higher dimensions! In 2 dimensions there are 17 space groups while in 3 dimensions there are 230.

Mathematicians do this sort of thing all the time. They seldom worry about the world we live in, and let their minds wander. In the process they discover many things. Later, (smart) physicists find that the results they need have already been found by mathematicians and tucked away in some corner (see Box 3.3)! Usually these results are disguised and not readily usable by the physicist. He has to 'shape it up' a bit, maybe, and then he is all ready to go. So bone up on your maths, and, more important, learn how to hunt for buried treasures! It will not only save your time, but also help you in a number of ways. The well-known physicist Eugene Wigner has a cryptic phrase to summarise all this: The unreasonable effectiveness of mathematics!

Back to symmetry breaking. How does it operate in liquid crystals? Compared to a crystal, only partially. Let us take the nematic as an example. We take the centre of mass of each molecule to denote its position. In the nematic, these positions are distributed at random, as in a liquid. Now in a normal liquid, e.g. liquid argon, I can move the atoms around randomly without, of course, bouncing into other atoms. What about the nematic liquid crystal? Well, here I can certainly allow the molecular positions to assume arbitrary distributions, *subject to the constraint that the molecules are all parallel to each other*. In the language of symmetry, the nematic has continuous translational symmetry but only partial rotational symmetry. Why only partial? Because when I perform rotations about an axis parallel to the molecular axis, there is invariance. However, there is no such invariance when I try to rotate about the x- or the y-axis (Fig.2.8 a). So in a nematic liquid crystal, continuous translational symmetry is not broken at all while continuous rotational symmetry

Box 3.3 Here is a famous example of the way physicists derive help from mathematics. Around 1915, Einstein was struggling to give shape to the *General Theory of Relativity*. What he desperately needed was the mathematics to describe the geometry of curved space. He then approached his mathematician friend Marcel Grossman and said: 'Grossman, you must help or I will go crazy!' Grossman was born in Hungary but had settled down in Zurich, Switzerland. It was Grossman's father who was responsible for Einstein's first job — as a clerk in the Swiss Patent Office. To return to the story, Grossman searched through the library in his University, and later said to Einstein: 'The geometry you are looking for has already been developed by Riemann.' Armed with this tool, Einstein could now make rapid progress. This story is narrated by Abraham Pais in his well-known book *Subtle is The Lord* which is a biography of Einstein. Pais heard the story from Einstein himself!

is preserved only about one direction. We can also say the same thing in terms of the number of *degrees of freedom*! None of the 3 translational degrees of freedom are affected by symmetry breaking when a liquid orders into a nematic liquid crystal but 2 rotational degrees of freedom are. Table 3.1 comprehensively tells the story.

Table 3.1 Symmetry breaking in various systems

System	No. of degrees affected		No. not affected	
	Translational	Rotational	Translational	Rotational
Liquid	0	0	3	3
Nematic	0	2	3	1
Smectic	1	2	2	1
Crystal	3	3	0	0

3.5 The first-order business!

Earlier, I mentioned in passing something about a first-order transition. Many important transitions in Nature *are* of the first-order type, and we simply can't ignore them. Nevertheless, physicists are guilty of giving first-order transitions a bit of a step-motherly treatment. This is mainly because of some exciting things that happen near T_C during a second-order transition. That story follows in the next Chapter, but first I must introduce you briefly to the idea of 'order' of a phase transition.

Basically, a phase transition indicates a discontinuous change in the state of ordering of the system. These changes can be of various types, each with its own characteristic signature. As an example, consider a gas. If it is a perfect gas obeying the well-known Boyle's law, the pressure versus volume curve would be as shown in Fig.3.8(a). Real gases, when compressed, go over into the liquid state by a first-order transition, whence the P–V diagram is as in (b). If, for some reason, the transition were to be of the second order, the diagram would be as in (c). Based on such characteristics, physicists have detailed criteria for labelling the order of a transition.

Let us now look at a first-order transition in the Landau style. Instead of eqn (3.1) we now have

$$F = a(T - T_C)\,\psi^2 + b\,\psi^4 + c\,\psi^3 \qquad a,b > 0,\ \ c < 0 \tag{3.5}$$

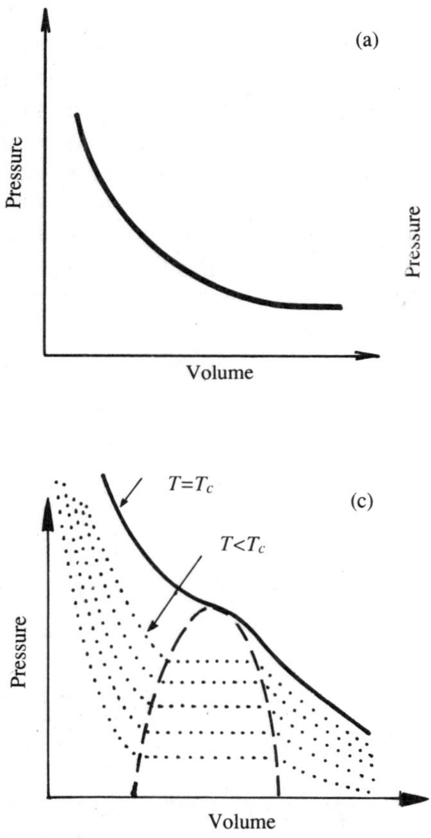

Fig.3.8 (a) *P–V* curve for an ideal gas, i.e. one obeying Boyle's law. Such a gas always remains a gas, no matter how much it is compressed and/or cooled. It is a one-phase system. Real gases, when (cooled and) compressed sufficiently, condense into the liquid phase via a first-order transition. The *P–V* curve in this case would look like (b). For a second-order transition, the curve would look like the solid line in (c). This curve can be looked upon as the limit, when the temperature is varied, of the dashed lines which are similar to the curve in (b). The transition occurs at a critical temperature T_c.

A new fellow has appeared — the cubic term $c\psi^3$. This makes the free energy curves look rather different (Fig.3.9). The curves in the figure are all asymmetrical, but even so, above T_t (— to show we are dealing with the first order, we shall use the notation T_t to denote the transition temperature which, however, is related to T_c occurring in (3.5)), the minimum of the free energy occurs at $\psi = 0$. At $T = T_t$, there are two minima, both with $F = 0$. This means that the system can either choose $\psi = 0$ or $\psi = \psi_1$. Nature takes advantage of this and forms small pockets where $\psi = \psi_1$ instead of being zero as elsewhere. These pockets are sometimes called nuclei, and their formation is referred to as *nucleation*. If T is lowered slightly below T_t, the minima with $\psi \neq 0$ offers slightly lower free energy. So all the nuclei rapidly grow, link up with each other and order prevails throughout. Ordering thus occurs essentially by a *nucleation and growth process*. By contrast, in a second-order transition, ordering occurs everywhere simultaneously, as if at one stroke.

3.6 On quasi crystals

Remember I said something about a 'package deal' between rotations and translations when a liquid becomes a crystal? Thanks to this deal, certain rotations are never allowed. For example, a two-dimensional crystal with 5-fold rotational symmetry is not possible. There is nothing mysterious about this. If you are mathematically inclined and know your trigonometry, you can prove it yourself. Another way is to cut out of cardboard, identical *regular* pentagons (all sides equal, all angles equal), spread them on a table, and try to fit them together (like in a jig-saw puzzle), without gaps. You will find that you can't avoid gaps (Fig.3.10)!

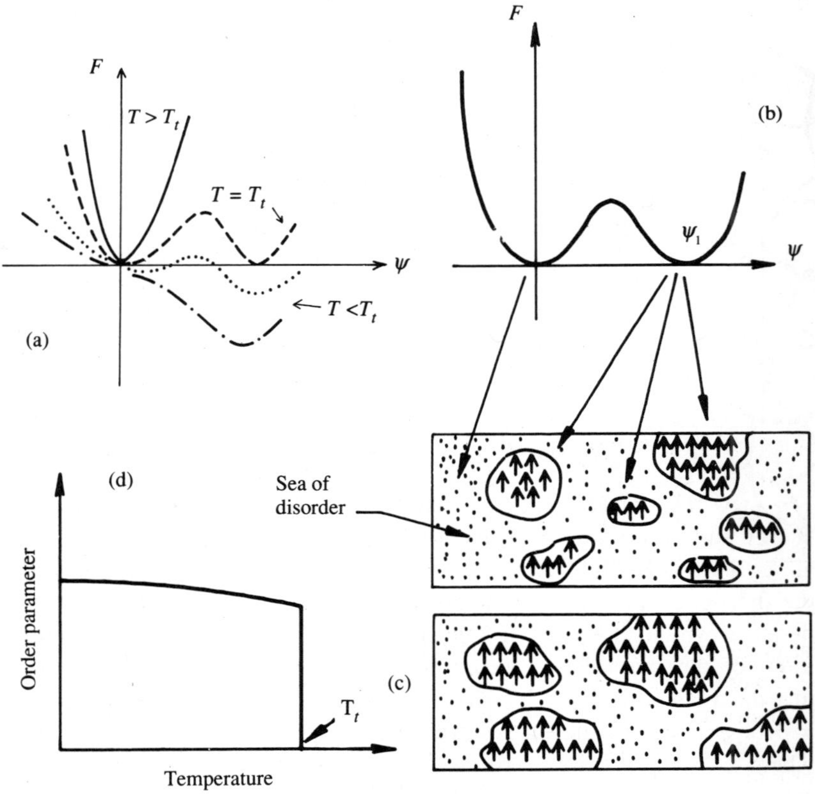

Fig.3.9 (a) A plot of F as defined in eqn (3.5) for various temperatures. For $T > T_t$ the transition temperature, the minimum is at $\psi = 0$; so there is no order. At $T = T_t$, there are two minima one of which is at $\psi \neq 0$. Nature takes advantage of this and allows small ordered regions to nucleate in a sea of disorder as shown in (b). In time, these ordered regions grow as in (c) and eventually link up. If T is even slightly less than T_t, then the minima with $\psi \neq 0$ is lower in energy and the ordered state is the only one allowed. A plot of the order parameter with temperature (d) shows a discontinuity at T_t. Compare with Figs.2.9 and 3.2.

So all this led to a dogma: When a liquid orders into a solid, it *cannot* have 5-fold rotational symmetry (recall remarks on p.38). Seems OK, and there is no reason to doubt it. Forget ordering, liquids etc., for the moment and let us turn to Roger Penrose, a brilliant mathematical physicist. Penrose works on exotic things like black holes, as does the famous Chandrasekhar (see *Chandrasekhar and His Limit*). You would think that a person like him who must be concentrating so hard would seek relaxation in music, painting or sports. Penrose probably does pursue all these but he also does puzzles for relaxation! He once asked: Can we tile the floor (i.e. without gaps and overlaps) in an orderly manner so that the tiling pattern has 5-fold rotational symmetry? Obviously we can't do it with a single type of tile (as Fig.3.10 shows); but is it possible with more than one kind of tile, and if

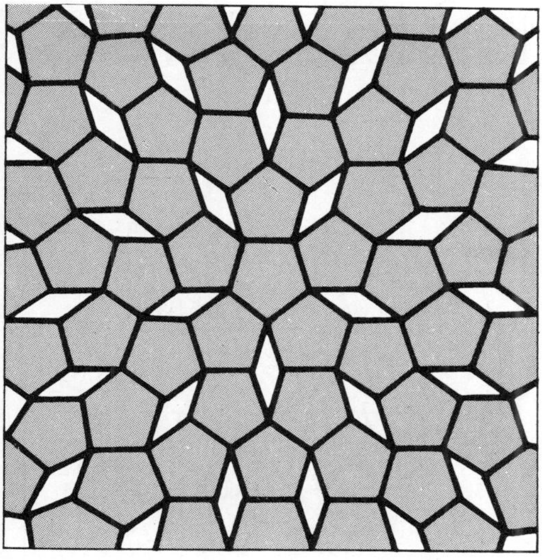

Fig.3.10 If one tries to tile the plane with regular pentagons, one will find that there are gaps which cannot be filled. This exercise proves that it is impossible to have a *periodic* structure (in two dimensions) with 5-fold rotational symmetry. Penrose proved that 5-fold rotational symmetry *was* possible, provided one gave up (i) *periodic* tiling, and (ii) allowed more than one unit cell, see Fig.3.11.

so, what is the minimum number of tile types required? Penrose found that given two types of tiles, this tiling problem could be solved and that there were in fact many solutions (i.e. tiling patterns). Two of these are shown in Fig.3.11. Soon after Penrose found these solutions, Martin Gardner wrote about it in the *Scientific American*, and drew the attention of the world to the *Penrose tilings*. At this stage it was still an amusement exercise, with people wondering: How would my bathroom look if I decorated it with Penrose tiling?

In 1984, some metallurgists at the National Bureau of Standards in Washington discovered that an alloy of aluminium and manganese which they had made had a 3-dimensional Penrose tiling structure! In particular, this alloy had the forbidden 5-fold rotational symmetry!! The alloy was

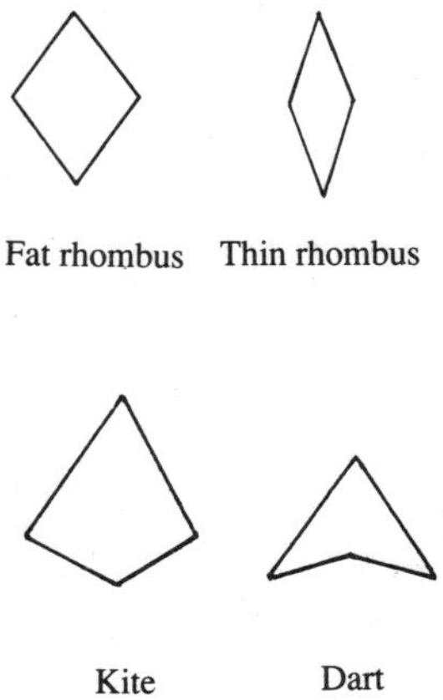

(a)

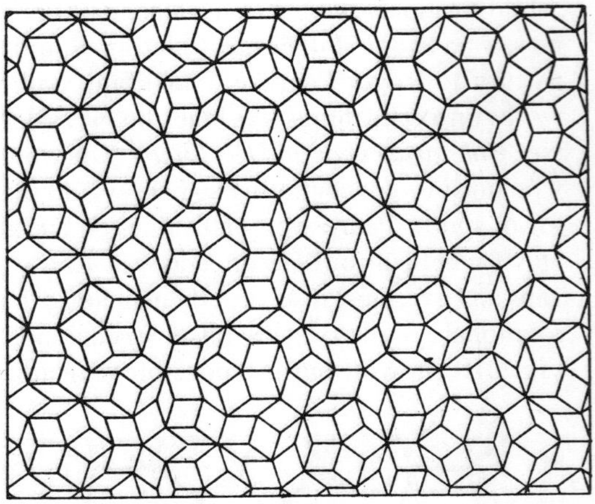

(b)

Fig.3.11 Two examples of Penrose tiling. The patterns are quasi-periodic, and built up using two tile types as in (a). Pattern (b) is made up of fat and thin rhombuses, while pattern (c) is made using the kite and the dart. These patterns were prepared by my colleague G. Athithan using a computer. Notice pattern (c) has been autographed by Penrose! Though not quite evident, the Penrose tiling *does* have 5-fold rotational symmetry; this is more clearly evident in a diffraction pattern. See Fig.3.12.

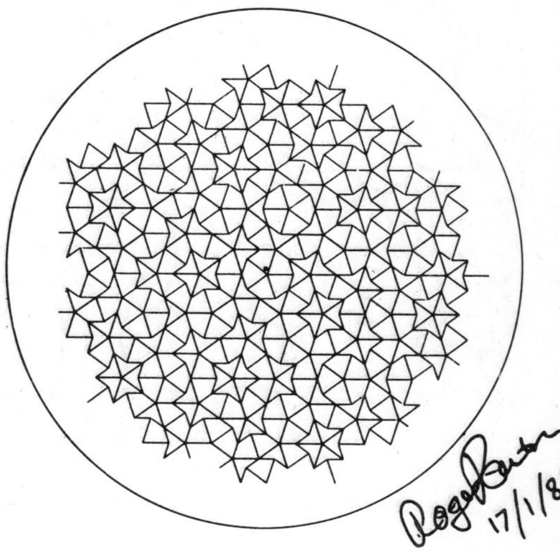

(c)

ordered, but it was not a crystal — it couldn't be, since mathematics prohibited it! Clearly this alloy of Al–Mn had to be something else. It was identified as a *quasi crystal*. This is the crystallographer's name for Penrose tiling.

A crystal has periodicity which makes it an ordered system. Periodicity prohibits 5-fold symmetry. A quasi crystal has quasi-periodicity which lends order. Quasi-periodicity *does not* forbid 5-fold rotational symmetry. Till 1984, physicists had not thought of quasi-periodicity and somehow they assumed it did not exist in the physical world. Well, there was a surprise in store for them!

Fig.3.12 Electron diffraction pattern of an alloy of aluminium and manganese. This picture was made at the Indira Gandhi Centre for Atomic Research. The spots have the required 5-fold rotational symmetry. For more details concerning electron diffraction, see Box 3.5.

Quasi-periodicity is a bit difficult to describe. I have attempted an explanation in Box 3.4. The essential point is this: When there is (translational) ordering, there is a definite rule for placing the tiles. The rules are different for a crystal and a quasi crystal. What we should note here is that quasi crystal tiling *also* has rules. The second point — crystals can be built with just one type of tile (called the unit cell), whereas, quasi crystals require a minimum of *two* distinct unit cells. Remember, quasi crystals also are translationally ordered, *even though they are not periodic.*

3.7 Magnetic ordering

What about magnets? What symmetries do they break? When an atom has a spin, it is almost as if it possessed an extra pair of hands! The physicist would be more formal and declare that the atom has extra degrees of freedom. What it means is that the spins could possibly organise themselves to suit their own convenience. Of course the spins are 'tied' to the atoms and they jolly well have to be where the atoms are. But how they point is their own business. If the spins have only two possible orientations, e.g. up and down, then the spins have only 1 degree of (spin orientational) freedom. If they can point in any direction in a plane (like the arms of a clock), they have 2 degrees of freedom. The most general case of course is when they have 3 degrees of freedom and can point in any direction in space.

On the basis of all this, we can say that a ferromagnet breaks *spin rotational symmetry*. Other spin patterns in Fig.2.12 represent more complex symmetry breakings, involving both spin rotations and spin translations.

Magnetic lattices are described by what are now called *magnetic space groups*. These too were discovered by mathematicians much before physicists came up with spin patterns as shown in Fig.2.12.

Box 3.4 I shall illustrate here the difference between periodicity and quasi-periodicity by considering a 1-dimensional example. We must remember two things:

(i) Periodic as well as quasi-periodic sequences are both built according to definite rules, and
(ii) a periodic sequence can be built up with just one unit cell, whereas a quasi-periodic one requires a minimum of two.

Figure (a) shows a periodic sequence built up with long (L) tiles. To build a quasi-periodic sequence, we make replacements according to the following rules:

(i) Replace L by S, L and
(ii) replace S by L.

The first few sequences generated by the above replacement rules are shown; all these are periodic sequences. If replacements are repeated an infinite number of times, one will obtain a 1-dimensional quasi-periodic chain. This is a *Penrose tiling* in 1 dimension.

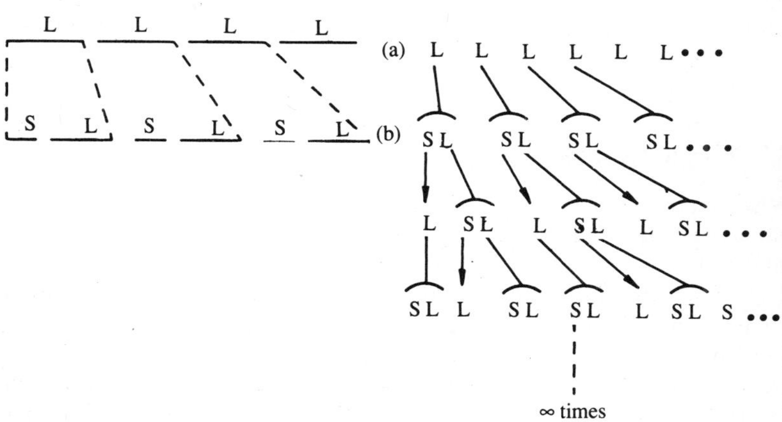

3.8 Fluctuations and symmetry breaking

Remember I said something earlier about the system randomly choosing between $+\psi_0$ and $-\psi_0$ when it orders? This requires further comment.

When a system tries to order, it usually has many patterns of ordering to choose from. For example, see Fig 2.11 (b), (c), (d). Of these, the system

Box 3.5 Electron diffraction is similar to neutron diffraction described in Box 2.4. Like neutrons, electrons are also particles but, once again like neutrons, they have a wave-like character too. This is the wave-particle duality of the quantum world. To perform an electron diffraction experiment, one first produces a sharp beam of electrons similar to the one which impinges on the TV screen and produces a picture. Only, the energy is very much higher, $\sim 10^5$ eV or even more. The beam then passes through a thin slice of the material investigated. There it is diffracted by the atoms, and the diffracted beams produce spots on the photographic plate.

An electron microscope is somewhat similar to an electron diffraction apparatus. What is the difference? Sometimes one obtains diffraction *rings* instead of spots. When and why? Try to find out! Also, what is the problem in making a neutron microscope?

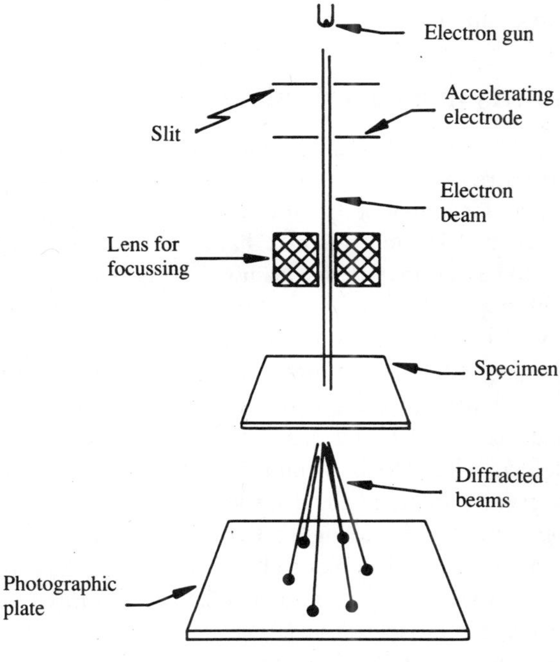

randomly chooses one, provided there are no biasing external forces, like an external magnetic field for example.

How come the choice is random? An example will make it clear. Consider the marble in Fig.3.13. It is delicately poised, and clearly in a

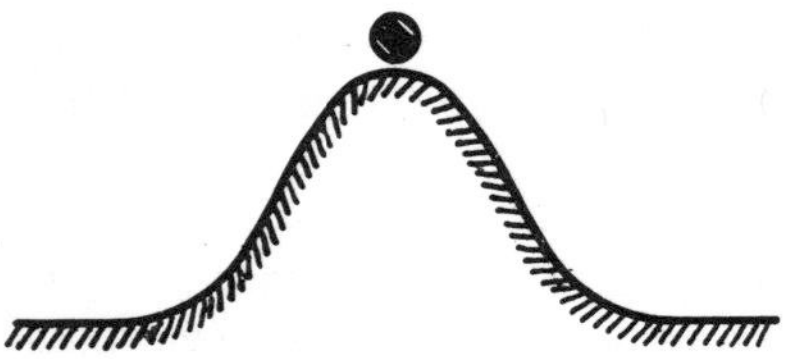

Fig.3.13 Marble in unstable equilibrium. Slightest disturbance, and it will roll down one side or the other to a more stable equilibrium. The choice between the left and the right is random.

state of unstable equilibrium. The slightest disturbance, and it will roll down one side or the other. The disturbance could be due to someone banging the door, a sudden gust of wind or something like that. We know for certain that whatever be the source of disturbance, the marble will definitely roll down; but we cannot predict which way it will.

The same is true of ordering during a phase transition. There are many choices, and one of these is picked at random. Which particular one depends on the fluctuations acting on the system. So maybe we should learn something about fluctuations near the transition temperature. This we shall do in Chapter 4.

3.9 Symmetry and imperfections

You might have seen young mothers putting a black spot on the face of their baby after dressing it up nicely. The idea seems to be to deliberately spoil the beauty a bit so that people looking at the child do not feel jealous and cast an evil eye! We may dismiss that as superstition but curiously, Nature seems to behave in the same fashion!! What I mean is that ordered states are seldom perfect and that there are always defects in them.

Now the ordering in a system can be spoilt in many ways. One could tear the system, smash it and so forth. All this will undoubtedly produce defects but these would be arbitrary defects. The defects that Nature introduces during the ordering process are 'planned' defects; rather I should say defects related to the symmetries of the parent, i.e. the ordered state and the grand parent, i.e. the disordered state. Pundits refer to such defects as *topological* defects. Figure 3.14 shows an example.

Defects can have their own hierarchies. To understand this, consider the lattice in Fig.3.15(a). This is perfect. That in Fig.3.15(b) has a defect called a *vacancy*, i.e. a missing atom. (A vacancy is not a topological defect but will do for illustrating the point I am presently making.) Under certain

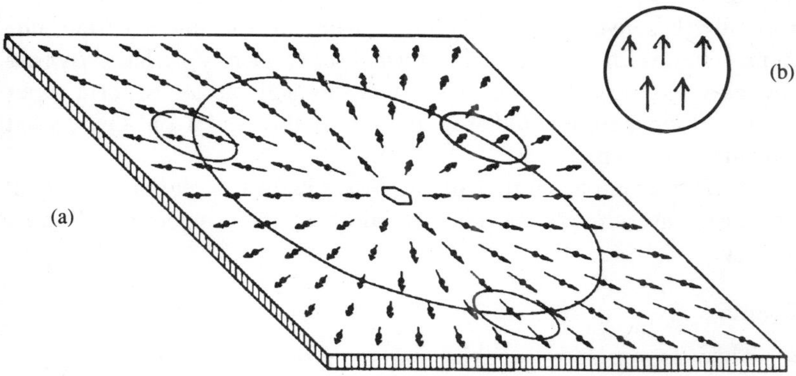

Fig.3.14 Topological defect in a 2-D spin system. Remember, the system is infinite! Although the spins appear to radiate from a point (which, incidentally, is called a singularity), in small patches the spins all appear to be parallel to each other as in (b). The defect is thus a collage of locally-ordered regions.

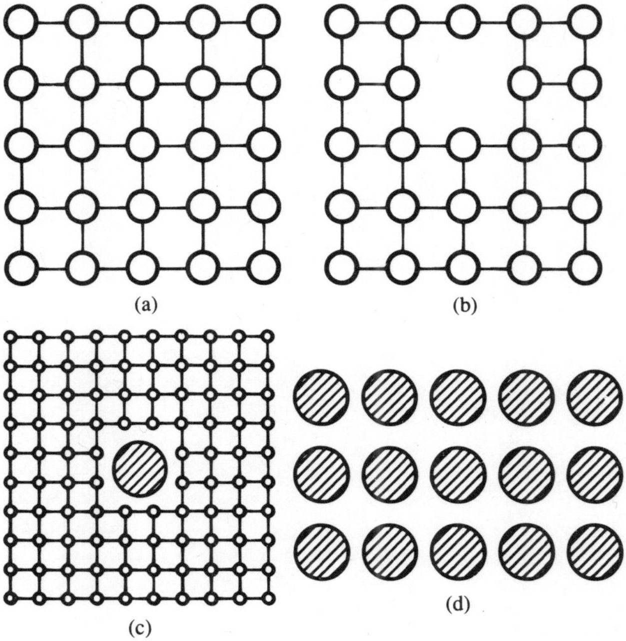

Fig.3.15 (a) A perfect 2-D lattice and (b) shows one with a vacancy. A collection of vacancies leads to a *void* as shown in (c). If there are many voids, they could, under certain circumstances, themselves form a lattice as in (d). One could now visualise a vacancy in a void lattice, supervoids formed by such supervacancies and so on!

conditions, vacancies could come together to form a larger defect called *void* as in Fig.3.15(c). Of course several voids could be formed, and normally these would be randomly distributed. But under certain circumstances, voids get ordered to form a *void lattice*. Void lattices could now have vacancies of their own which can agglomerate to form super voids, and super voids could order to form a lattice and so on! This is what I mean by defect hierarchy.

Not many examples of such hierarchy are known as yet but theoretical physicists have already started studying them. The subject is still in its infancy.

To sum up :

- There is symmetry breaking during an order-disorder transformation.
- The symmetry of the broken-symmetry state is a subgroup of the symmetry of the disordered state.
- Topological defects possible in the ordered state are dependent on the nature of the symmetry of the ordered state
- Defects can order and also have a hierarchy.

4 *The Birth Pangs*

4.1 Excess specific heat

Look at Fig.4.1. This shows the specific heat of ammonium chloride and liquid helium. No two substances could be as widely different. Both undergo a second-order phase transition, and what you see in the figure is the specific heat in the neighbourhood of the transition temperature.

You probably know what specific heat is. It is the amount of heat required to raise the temperature of 1 gm of the substance through 1 °C. You would probably prefer SI units! Anyway, what is more interesting is that the specific heat shoots up near the transition temperature T_c.

Specific heat tells us something about the 'internal freedom' of a system. An analogy may help. Consider the two vessels in Fig.4.2. The water level in both vessels is the same, but one is wide while the other is narrow. We shall assume that raising the level of the water is like raising the temperature. We now pour water in both vessels so that in each case the water level rises by 1 cm. Clearly we have to pour more water in the wider vessel because the water has plenty of room to spread around. In the same way, more internal freedom implies greater specific heat.

What is this internal freedom and how does it become large near T_c? Internal freedom in the present case refers to the many different ways in which the order parameter can fluctuate near T_c.

Earlier when we were talking of ordering, order parameter, etc., we made one very simple assumption (although I didn't tell you about it !) namely, that there are no fluctuations. In the disordered state, $\Psi = 0$, and in the ordered state ψ has the same value everywhere which does not change with time. This is not true. If we look into the material at a temperature just above T_c (we shall write this as T_c^+) we will observe something close to what is shown in Fig.4.3. There are little groups of ordered spins, some big and some small. Isn't this the same as what happens during a first-order transition (recall Fig.3.9)? Not quite, for here the clusters of the ordered region form, break up, form again, break up again and so on. Thus, clusters keep appearing and disappearing, i.e. they are evanescent. You might have seen this sort of thing in a crowd near an accident site. People form little groups and talk. The groups then break up, other groups form and so on.

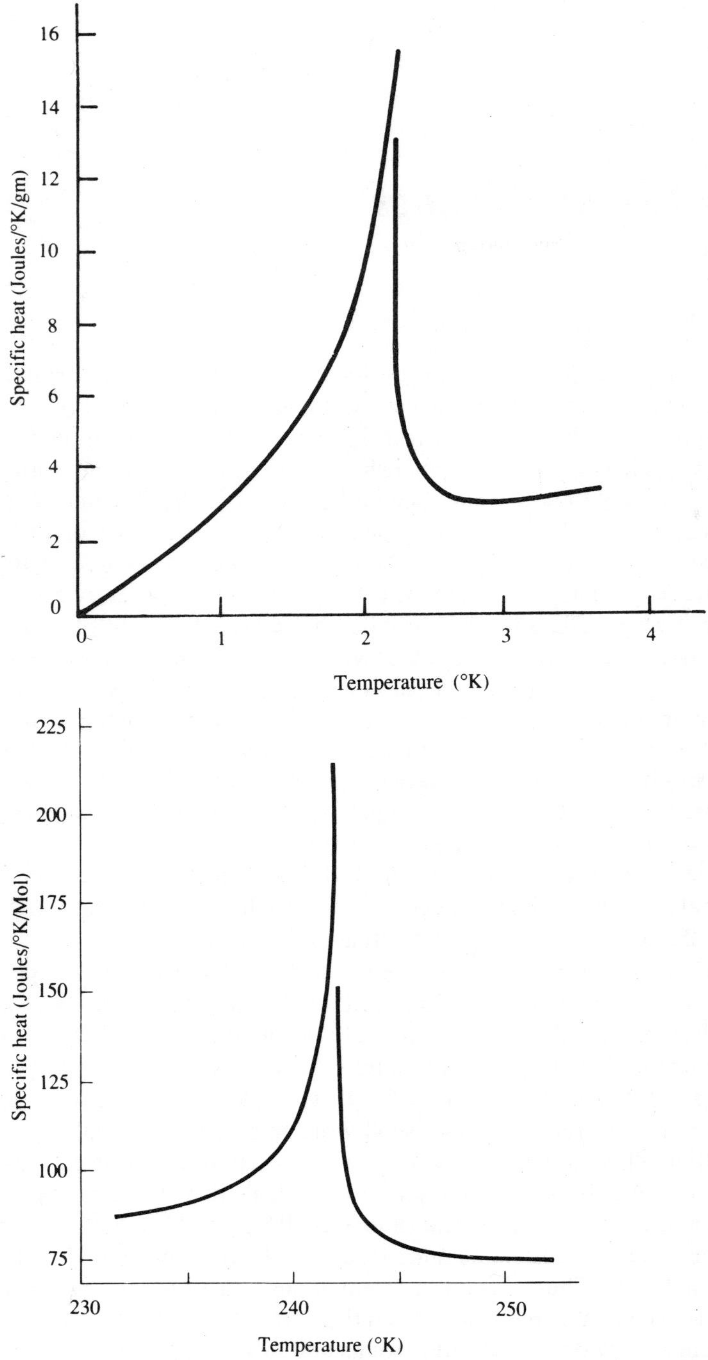

Fig.4.1 Specific heat curves for liquid helium and ammonium chloride near their transition temperatures.

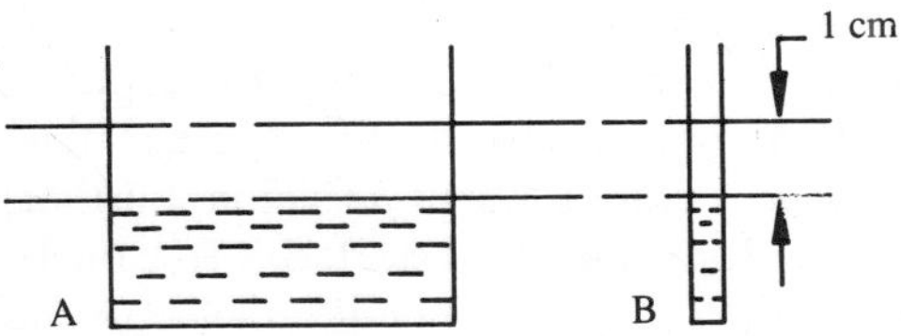

Fig.4.2 A and B are two vessels with the same water level. To raise the level by 1 cm, we must obviously pour more water into A than into B. More water is like more specific heat. Specific heat becomes large when there is greater 'internal freedom'.

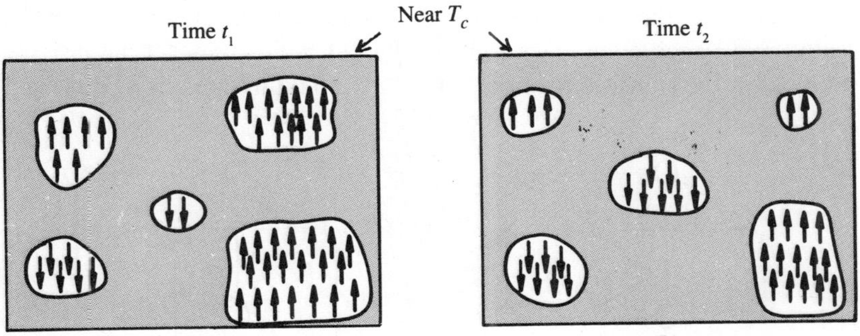

(a) (b)

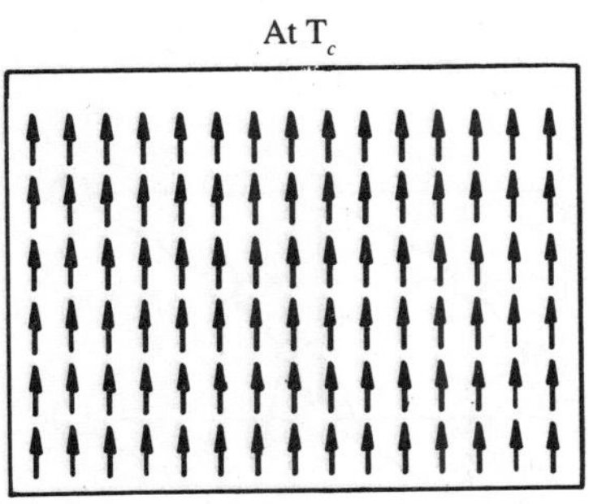

(c)

Fig.4.3 Pockets of ordering near T_c^+(see a and b). The shaded portion represents the disordered region. Observe firstly that both positive and negative (or up and down) clusters can form, and secondly that cluster patterns are different at different times. At T_c, one large cluster (randomly formed) tilts the balance and causes symmetry breaking (see c).

The formation of ordered clusters represents order parameter fluctuations. The specific heat experiments tell us that such fluctuations are vigorous close to T_c. The sizes of these clusters vary as also their lives. If you prefer jargon you could say the order parameter has spatio-temporal fluctuations!

4.2 Identical birth pangs

OK. So we have these order parameter fluctuations which contribute to excess specific heat. I would now like to draw your attention to another aspect of this specific heat business. But before I do that, I must say something about the ordering that takes place in ammonium chloride (NH_4Cl) and that which occurs in liquid helium. A portion of the ammonium chloride lattice is shown in Fig. 4.4. The unit cell is cubical, and sitting inside each cube is an ammonium (NH_4^+) ion. Below T_c all the ions are oriented the same way whereas above T_c the ions randomly choose between the two possible orientations for the ion. For chemical bonding, a NH bond must necessarily point towards a Cl^- ion. Further, the tetrahedral structure of the NH_4^+ ion cannot be distorted. So the phase transition in NH_4Cl is connected with the *orientational ordering* of the NH_4^+ ions.

What about the transition in liquid helium? This is a bit more complicated and I shall come back to it in Chapter 5. For now, let me just say that below the transition temperature 2.2 °K, helium remains a liquid and

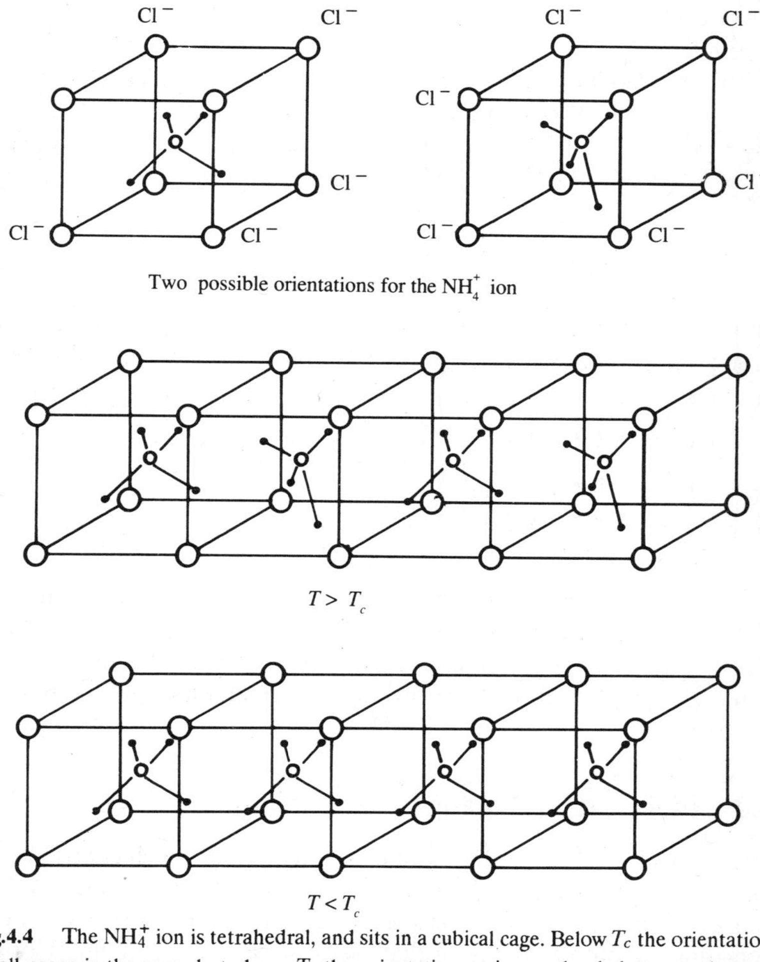

Fig.4.4 The NH_4^+ ion is tetrahedral, and sits in a cubical cage. Below T_c the orientation in all cages is the same but above T_c the orientation varies randomly between the two possibilities, from cube to cube.

visually appears the same. However, the liquid acquires unusual flow properties. The low-temperature phase is therefore called the *superfluid* phase. More about this in Chapter 5. The superfluidity is caused by the emergence of what maybe called quantum order or quantum discipline. Don't worry — I shall try to unravel some of this mystery later. For the moment let us accept that in superfluid liquid helium, the order parameter is a complex number and that critical phenomena are associated with the fluctuations of this somewhat unusual order parameter which is quantum mechanical in origin. I can't draw pretty pictures as in Fig.4.3, but you must accept that fluctuations of the order parameter occur also in liquid helium. That is the only way we can explain the specific heat peak. By the way, observe that the specific heat curve looks like the Greek letter lambda (λ). People therefore sometimes refer to this as the λ-transition.

Observe a remarkable fact. The nature of the orderings in NH_4Cl and that in liquid helium are *quite different*. And yet the specific heat curves look similar! In fact, if we plot the two graphs suitably, they will lie almost smack on top of each other. Figure 4.5 shows how to do this. First we switch to a *reduced temperature t* defined by

$$t = \frac{T - T_c}{T_c}$$

What it means is simply this: In the case of helium (T_c = 2.2°K), when T = 3°K, then, instead of 3°K, I write $t \sim 0.36$. Notice that since t is defined as temperature difference divided by temperature, it is just a number, i.e. it has no dimensions.

When I employ a reduced temperature scale, the two specific heat curves appear as in Fig. 4.5(b). The breaks appear in the same place but the curves are vertically displaced. I can now scale the specific heat to either move the helium curve up or bring the NH_4Cl curve down (Fig. 4.5c).

So we discover this remarkable thing. The order that occurs in these two systems is widely different and yet the curves for the excess specific heat look the same! How does this happen? Crudely speaking, what it means is that *the birth pangs are the same no matter what is being born*! Experts would rather say that there is *Universality in critical phenomena.*

4.3 Critical phenomena and exponents

Universality is big business. Theoretical physicists explore it with ingenious models while experimentalists try either to prove or even disprove theorists with clever experiments. Before I discuss that, I must tell you that *critical phenomenon* is not a new thing; it has been known for close to a hundred years.

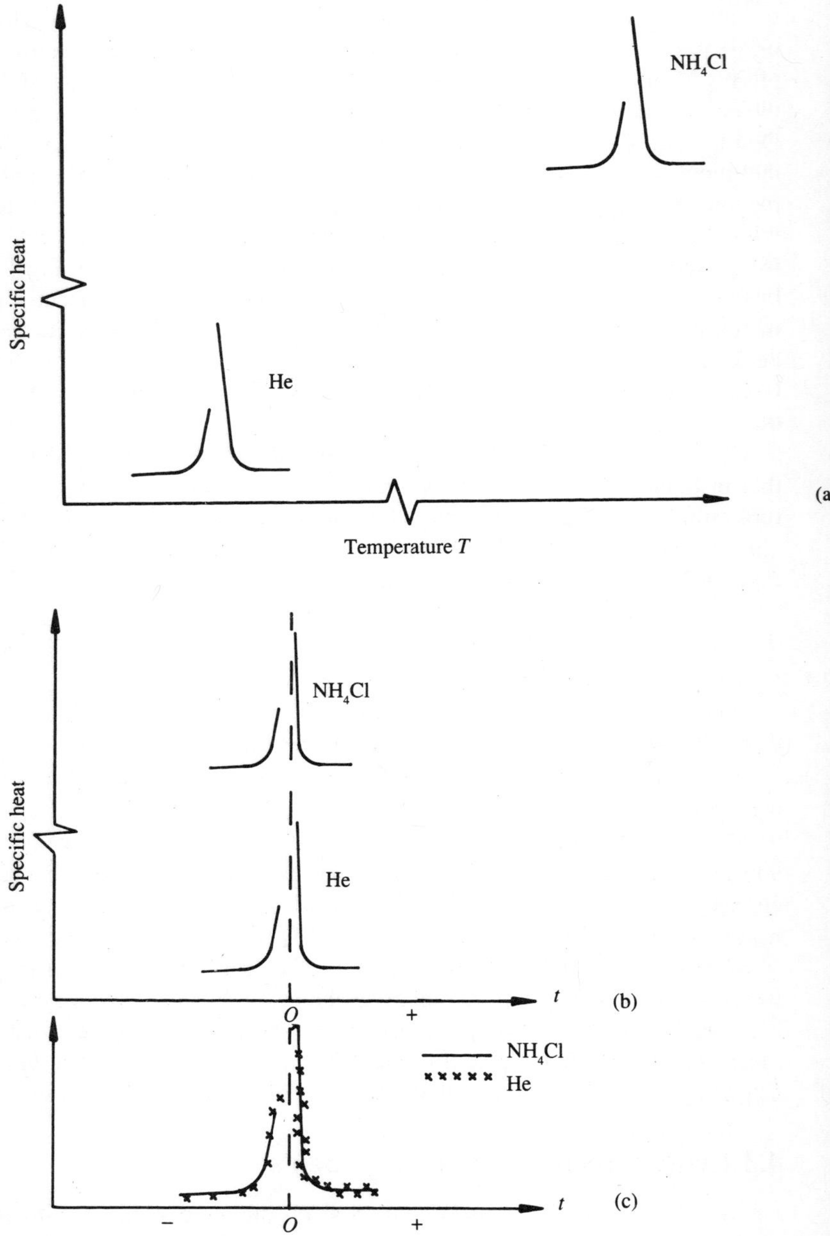

Fig.4.5 (a) Schematic specific heat curves for NH_4Cl and liquid helium in their usual forms; (b) shows the curves after the temperature scale is changed to the reduced temperature scale; (c) shows the specific heat curves after vertical scaling.

There is a simple way of demonstrating it. Pour some cyclohexane in a test tube, and then some acetic anhydride on top of it. The two liquids do not mix at room temperature and so the lighter liquid will float. A clear meniscus will be present, indicating the separation of the two liquids. Now heat the test tube. When heated sufficiently, the two liquids will mix completely. Now let the test tube cool slowly. As the temperature approaches 53.4 °C, you will find that the liquid in the tube begins to appear milky white. This whitishness keeps increasing for a while and then dies down. At this stage the contents of the test tube become clear again, but by now the two liquids have separated, and the dividing meniscus would again be clearly visible. The temperature 53.4 °C marks the *miscibility transition* in the binary liquid system and the whitish appearance near the transition temperature is referred to as *critical opalescence*. It arises on account of light scattering by order parameter fluctuations or *critical fluctuations* as they are called. Incidentally, light scattering is a good technique to use for studying critical phenomena – in optically transparent materials of course!

In 1912, Einstein and the Polish scientist Smoluchowski explained critical opalescence for the first time. They rightly attributed it to fluctuations. Subsequently, many careful experiments were performed, and the theory also had to be improved.

Specific heat is not the only quantity of interest near a phase transition. There are several others, of which I should mention (i) the order parameter and (ii) the susceptibility.

Parents are always worried about young people being susceptible to bad influence! In physics, susceptibility is a measure of the response of the system to an applied force. This can be expressed as a general equation, i.e

$$\text{Response} = \text{susceptibility} \times \text{force} \qquad (4.1)$$

which means that susceptibility can be defined as the response to unit applied force. See Box 4.1 for further information.

The applied force can be a hydrostatic pressure, an electric field, or any other force. We would be interested in that force which would influence the order parameter, i.e. the response would be in terms of order, measured of course by the order parameter. The corresponding susceptibility is called the *order-parameter susceptibility*. In such cases as ferromagnetism, the applied force that would tickle the order parameter is easy to identify and produce in the laboratory. In this case the order parameter is the magnetization M and the applied force would have to be a magnetic field H. In the case of superfluid helium, one knows what the order parameter is but one does not have a way of generating the corresponding force in the lab. This is a problem only for the experimenter, and does not trouble theorists!

Anyway, we have these three quantities namely, the specific heat, the order parameter and the susceptibility, and we wish to know how they all vary in the critical region, i.e. as a function of the reduced temperature t. I should mention here that the present discussion concerns only second-order phase transitions, for it is only in these that the fluctuations are strong. The theoretical description of these fluctuations posed a major challenge that was answered only recently.

To get back to what I was saying, near T_C, the different quantities mentioned above vary as follows:

SPECIFIC HEAT
$$C \sim \frac{1}{t^{\alpha}} \qquad t > 0$$
$$\sim \frac{1}{(-t)^{\alpha'}} \qquad t < 0$$

ORDER PARAMETER
$$\psi \sim 0 \qquad t > 0$$
$$\sim \frac{1}{(-t)^{\beta}} \qquad t < 0$$

SUSCEPTIBILITY
$$\chi \sim \frac{1}{t^{\gamma}} \qquad t > 0$$
$$\sim \frac{1}{(-t)^{\gamma'}} \qquad t < 0$$

Box 4.1 The first thing to note about eqn (4.1) is that it defines what is called the *linear* susceptibility, meaning that the response depends on the first power of the applied force. Let us write eqn (4.1) as

$$R = \chi F$$

where χ is the linear susceptibility. Suppose R depends also on the higher powers of F, i.e.

$$R = \chi F + \chi^{(2)} F^2 + \chi^{(3)} F^3 + \ldots$$

Here $\chi^{(2)}$, $\chi^{(3)}$, ... are called nonlinear susceptibilities, with $\chi^{(2)}$ being of second order, $\chi^{(3)}$ of third order, and so on.

In eqn (4.1) it is implicitly assumed that the same force is applied everywhere and that we are looking for the overall or global response. Instead, one could apply the force at a point r and ask for the response at a different point r'. This would involve the *nonlocal* susceptibility $\chi(r, r')$. One could also apply the force at some time t and ask for the response at a *later* time t'. This would involve the *time-dependent susceptibility* $\chi(t, t')$. The most general case would be to apply the force at the point r at the time t and ask for the response at another point r' at a later time t'. This would involve the susceptibility $\chi(r, t; r', t')$.

Here ~ means *varies like*. Observe that variations are always like t to the power of something. Hence such variations are called *power laws*. The quantities α, β ..., etc., are referred to as *exponents*. Power laws usually imply interesting physics, and when they occur physicists get excited.

What are the numerical values of $\alpha, \beta, \gamma,$ etc? Landau's theory gives the following values:

$$\alpha = \alpha' = 0, \quad \beta = 0.5, \quad \gamma = \gamma' = 1.0 \tag{4.3}$$

Sometimes, these are also referred to as *mean field* theory results.

Very careful measurements made quite close to T_C have shown that the mean field values are not correct. That is, measurements have been

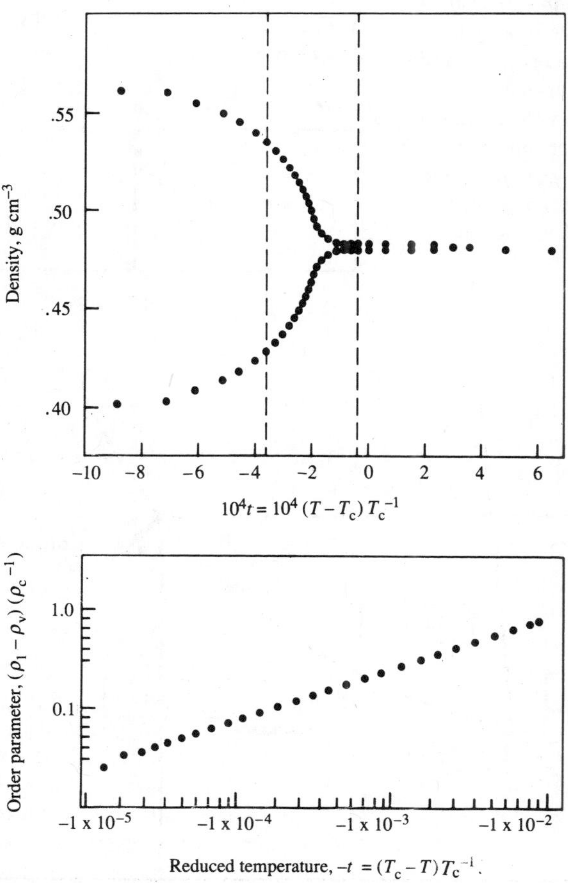

Fig.4.6 Order parameter for liquid neon as a function of t near the critical point for the fluid. Critical point is explained in Box 4.2. Both the order parameter and the reduced temperature are plotted on a logarithmic scale.

made at temperatures very close to T_c, such as $T = 0.99995\ T_c$ (Fig.4.6). To perform such experiments, the temperature must be held constant and uniform throughout the sample. All this is a great challenge, calling for much skill and ingenuity. So don't think that only theorists are smart!

Box 4.2 Figure (a) shows the phase diagram for a simple system like neon. (Try and relate it to Fig.1.3c). When a liquid is heated at constant pressure (e.g. atmospheric), its state varies along a horizontal line like the one shown. Boiling occurs when the line cuts the liquid–vapour phase boundary (e.g., point A). This is a first-order transition. Points A, B, . . . all mark first-order transitions. The phase boundary is thus the locus of first-order transition points. It ends at the critical point C corresponding to temperature T_c and pressure P_c. If the system is taken along the line OCBA, then a second-order transition occurs at C. Above T_c there is only vapour but below T_c the cell is filled partly with liquid (having density ρ_l) and partly with vapour (having density ρ_v). These vary as shown in (b). The order parameter is defined by $\psi = (\rho_l - \rho_v) / \rho_c$ where ρ_c is the density at T_c. It is this which is plotted in Fig.4.6.

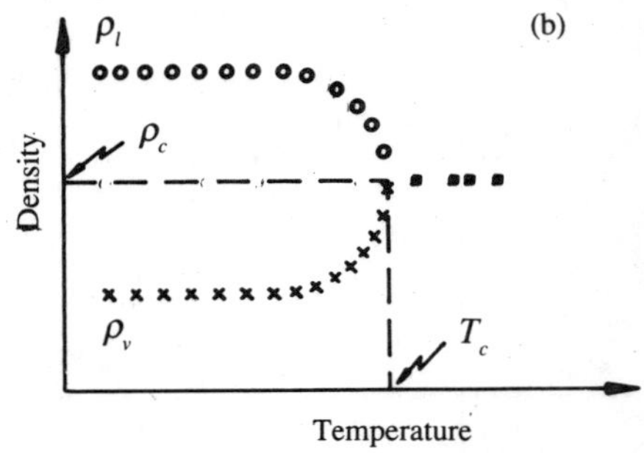

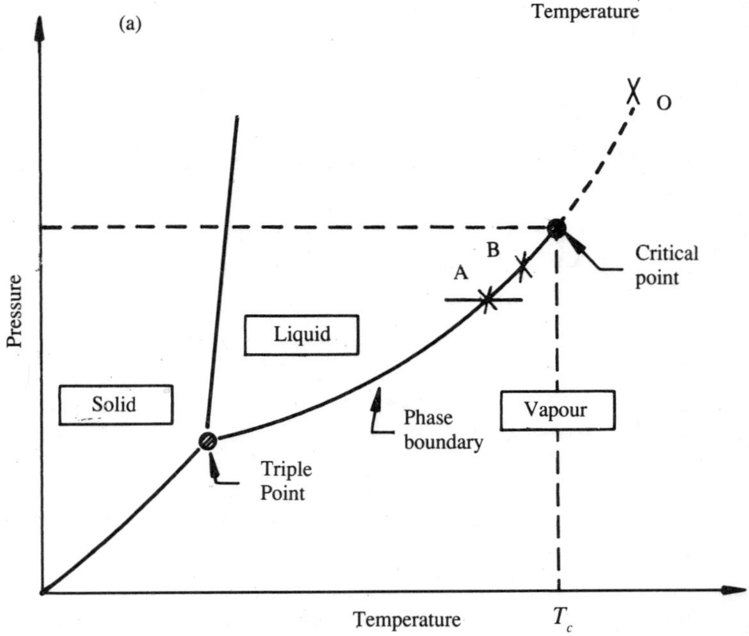

4.4 Beyond mean field theory

Careful experiments have shown two things: (i) Mean field values for the *critical exponents* α, β and γ are not correct, and (ii) there are several *Universality classes*. Let me take these one by one.

The fact that mean field values are incorrect is not surprising. In 1944, Lars Onsager of America studied a model 2-dimensional system of spins which could point either up or down. He not only proved that this system had a ferromagnetic phase transition, but he also calculated the critical exponents; the values all came out to be different from those predicted by the mean field theory. Careful experiments on various sytems in the sixties and the seventies reinforced this conclusion. Thereupon K. Wilson (see Box 4.3) developed a theory called the *renormalization group theory* (it is fashionable to simply call it (RNG) which predicted numbers for the critical exponents close to those observed.

> **Box 4.3** K. Wilson is the son of another scientist, E.B. Wilson Jr., who was mentioned in Chapter 1. In the early days of quantum mechanics, the senior Wilson wrote a book on the subject along with the famous chemist Linus Pauling. K. Wilson joined the California Institute of Technology (Caltech) in 1956 to do his Ph.D. In those days the fashionable subject was elementary particle physics (it still is!). But Wilson rebelled, and worked for a while on plasma physics. During that time he used to discuss his problems with the famous Chandrasekhar. His father had told him: 'When you go to Caltech, be sure to meet the two great physicists there namely, Feynman and Gell-Mann'. K. Wilson says that when he called on Feynman, the latter seemed to be gazing at the ceiling. He asked Feynman, 'Professor, what are you working on at present?' Feynman replied, 'Nothing!' Wilson then went to Gell-Mann and became his student. After working on plasmas for a while, he went back to particle physics. He got his degree in 1960, went to Europe and continued doing particle physics till 1963. Around that time he read Onsager's paper. He became interested in critical phenomena, and after sometime developed the RNG, using tricks he had learnt in particle physics. For this he received the Nobel Prize in 1982. Afterwards he became interested in computer languages, and started a project called the *Gibbs Project* for the development of a computer language superior to the widely-used FORTRAN.

Wilson's work also shed light on the Universality class business. People recognized that while dealing with critical phenomena, one must keep track of two things (i) the dimensionality of the system (denoted by the symbol *d*), and (ii) the dimensionality of the order parameter (denoted by the symbol *n*). You might ask: What do you mean by the dimensionality of the system? Don't we live in a 3-D world? Isn't that the dimensionality of the system? True, physical systems exist in a 3-D world, but they could behave as if they had a different dimensionality. For instance, a membrane could be conveniently viewed as a 2-dimensional system. Moreover, theoreticians are all the time inventing models with different dimensionalities. So we need not always take d to be 3.

We turn next to the quantity n. The dimensionality of the order parameter is the number of independent variables required to describe it. Thus, for a scalar order parameter, $n = 1$. A vector order parameter can have $n = 2$, $n = 3$ or even larger values. Physicists characterize systems by the combination (d,n).

One can now make a chart as in Fig.4.7. Each (d,n) combination represents a different Universality class. What it means is that each (d,n) combination has its own unique set of values for the critical exponents. Different physical systems having the same (d, n) value will have the same critical exponents – see Table 4.1. To use our lingo, not only do physical systems have birth pangs, but the *birth pangs are the same* (within the same Universality class of course!).

Table 4.1 Critical exponents for systems belonging to various Universality classes

System	(d, n)	α	β	γ
Mean field theory		0	0.5	1
Ising model (Onsager; exact)	(2, 1)	0	0.125	7/4
Ferromagnet (approx. theory)	(3, 3)	−0.1	0.36	1.38
Iron (expt)	(3, 3)	−0.09 ± 0.01	0.34 ± 0.02	1.32 ± 0.02
Fluid (approx.theory)	(3, 1)	0.11	0.325	1.24
Xenon (expt)	(3, 1)	0.08 ± 0.02	~ 0.33	1.23

I must here make a confession. Superfluid helium and ammonium chloride do not belong to the same Universality class, i.e. they do not share the same (d,n) numbers! However, unless one looks very close to T_C, their exponents appear the same. Figure 4.1 reflects similarity only at this level. In fact, in the beginning people recognized only this kind of similarity. It was only later that the finer aspects were discovered, making necessary improvements beyond the mean field theory.

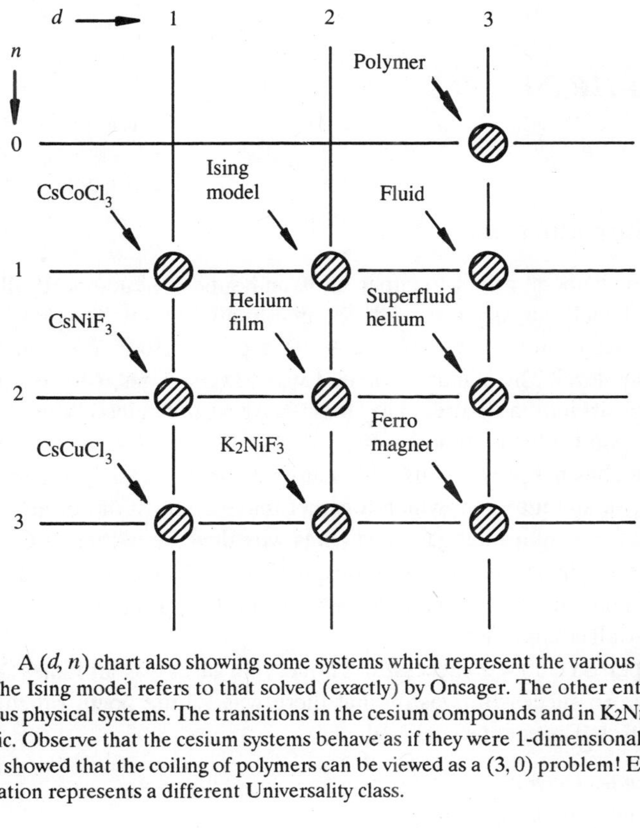

Fig.4.7 A (d, n) chart also showing some systems which represent the various combinations. The Ising model refers to that solved (exactly) by Onsager. The other entries refer to various physical systems. The transitions in the cesium compounds and in K_2NiF_3 are all magnetic. Observe that the cesium systems behave as if they were 1-dimensional. Prof. de Gennes showed that the coiling of polymers can be viewed as a (3, 0) problem! Each (d, n) combination represents a different Universality class.

To sum up :

- Fluctuations of the order parameter become very strong near T_C.
- Fluctuations lead to critical phenomena.
- Many properties show power law behaviour near T_C.
- Critical exponents are the same for all members belonging to the same universality class, i.e. the same (d, n) combination.
- Mean field theory is not adequate for predicting the values of the critical exponents. The RNG is required for doing this.

5 *The Supers*

5.1 Introduction

The term 'supers' refers to superfluids and superconductors. It all started with a Dutch physicist named Kammerlingh Onnes. Towards the end of the last century, there was a great race — How low can you go in temperature? The standard method was to take a gas, cool it somehow, and turn it into a liquid. The temperature so attained would be the boiling point of the liquid concerned.

Nature has not provided us with many (elemental) gases. Of course there are oxygen and nitrogen, which together make up most of our atmosphere. Both these are molecular gases, which is why they are written as O_2 and N_2. Chlorine and hydrogen are also molecular gases. Besides these there are the so-called rare gases namely, radon, xenon, krypton, argon, neon and helium. These are all atomic gases.

One person who was successful at liquefying gases was Sir James Dewar in England. So successful was he that there was a little poem ridiculing his competitors. The poem went like this:

Sir James Dewar
Is cleverer than you are
None of you asses
Can condense gases!

So, one by one all the gases (atomic and molecular) gave way until only two remained — hydrogen and helium. Later hydrogen was tamed (this brought the temperature record down to 22.4°K) and that left helium, standing alone and daring like Mount Everest! Finally, Onnes succeeded in liquefying helium in the early part of this century. A great milestone had been crossed, and the record book now showed 4.2°K as the lowest temperature attained. (For the march towards zero, see *A Hot Story*.)

Once a liquid was made, it was used as a refrigerant, that is, various solids would be placed in contact with the liquid so that they would attain the temperature of the liquid. The properties of the solid would then be studied at this temperature. When Kammerlingh Onnes liquefied helium, he too began to play this game. He had an advantage because he could command the lowest temperatures then available! Incidentally, the helium gas which Onnes used is supposed to have come from the monazite sands of Kerala – but that is another story.

Kammerlingh Onnes was studying how the electrical resistivity of mercury varies with temperature in the low temperature region. We know mercury as a liquid, but in Onnes' experiment it was a solid – naturally. Kammerlingh Onnes found that the electrical resistance of mercury varied as shown in Fig. 5.1. Below 4.1 °K the resistance *completely* vanished! This sort of thing was not known before. Zero resistance meant that current could flow without producing heat (remember, heat dissipated is given by I^2R) or in other words, electrons could flow through the metal without experiencing any friction. So the phenomenon was named *superconductivity*.

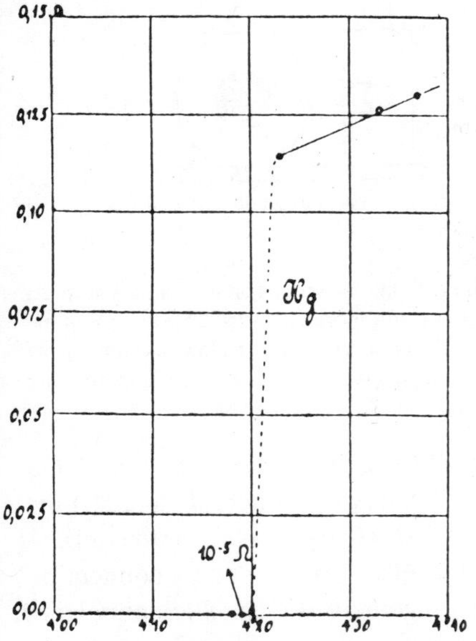

Fig.5.1 The original graph made by Kammerlingh Onnes in 1911 when he discovered superconductivity in solid mercury. The horizontal axis shows temperature in °K, and the vertical axis the electrical resistance in ohms. About the resistivity in the superconducting phase, Onnes wrote: ' ... the resistance was found to have fallen below 3×10^{-6} ohms, that is one ten-millionth of the value it would have at 0 °C '. The resistance actually vanishes in the superconducting phase, and any resistance one measures is due to the apparatus.

5.2 Superfluidity

In 1937, the great Soviet physicist Peter Kapitza (see Box 5.1, p.68) was studying the properties of liquid helium when it was cooled below 4.2 °K. How do you cool liquid helium? Very simple. Remember that when you climb up a mountain water boils at a temperature less than 100 °C? Why? Because the pressure on mountain tops is less than at sea level. The boiling point of water is 100 °C only at atmospheric pressure. In the same way, the boiling point of liquid helium is 4.2 °K only at atmospheric pressure. If we want to make it boil at a lower temperature then clearly we must reduce the pressure, as shown in Fig.5.2. Kapitza did just this and he found strange things happening below 2.2 °K.

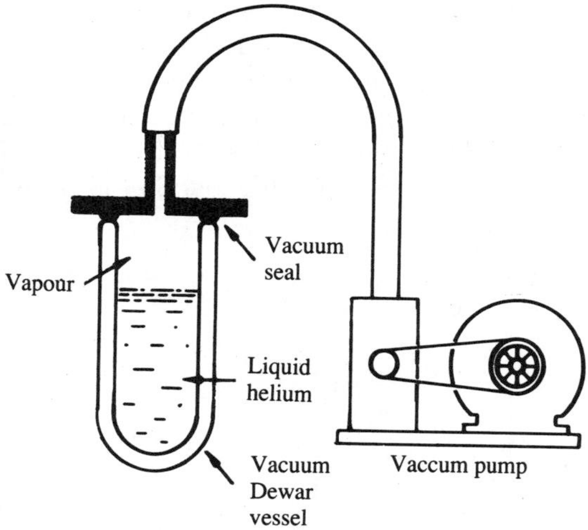

Fig.5.2 To reduce the temperature of liquid helium, one pumps on it as shown here. As the temperature is lowered, the liquid boils more and more vigorously. So the pump has to work very hard to keep the pressure down to the required value. The lowest temperature thus attainable obviously depends on the pumping capacity. It is not possible to go down below about 1 °K using this method.

It will take a whole book to describe all the fascinating things that happen in this low temperature phase. I can't do that here. Instead let me give you a couple of examples. Figure 5.3 shows two vessels, both containing liquid helium, but up to different levels. Kapitza made a connection between the two liquids using the arrangement shown. The connecting slit was made extremely narrow. It was found that above 2.2 °K liquid flowed from the inner vessel to the outer one with great difficulty. The levels did equalise, but only after a very long time. But below 2.2 °K, the equalisation occurred very rapidly. It seemed as if the liquid flowed without experiencing any friction (a better word would be viscosity), and so the phenomenon was named *superfluidity*.

Another example is illustrated in Fig.5.4. This is something the like of which you would never have seen before! All these strange goings on clearly pointed to a new and very unusual phase. And if a confirmation was needed that a phase transition had occurred, then the specific heat peak (recall Chapter 4) provided it.

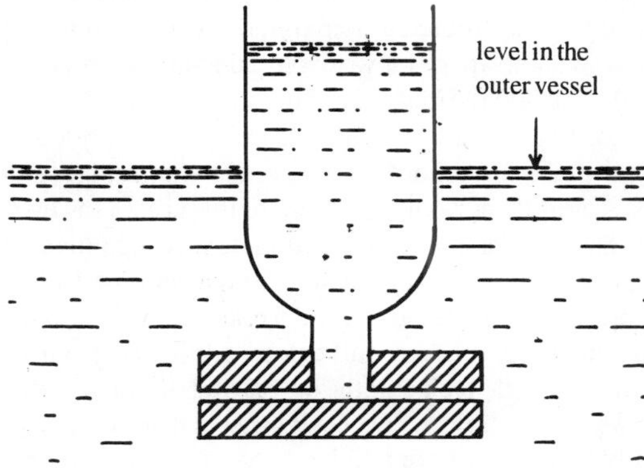

Fig.5.3 Liquid helium is filled in the inner and outer vessels, to different levels as shown. Naturally, the levels will try to equalise. Above the lambda transition, i.e., at 2.2°K, the equalisation takes a very long time but below, it happens in a jiffy!

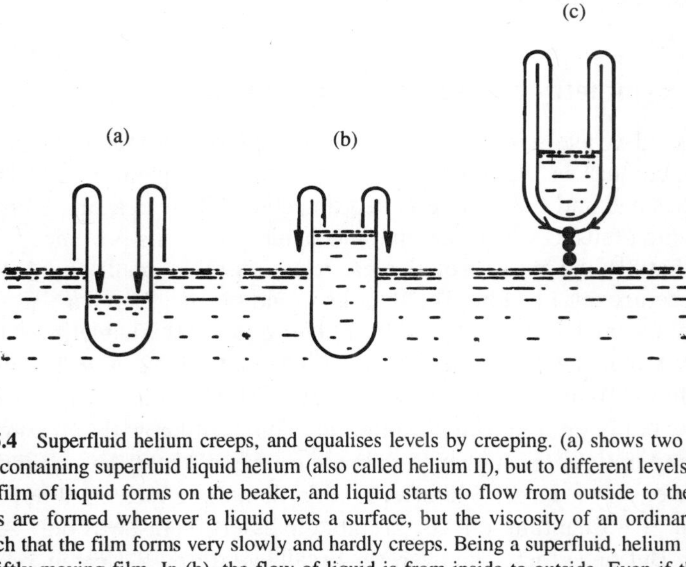

Fig.5.4 Superfluid helium creeps, and equalises levels by creeping. (a) shows two vessels, both containing superfluid liquid helium (also called helium II), but to different levels. A very thin film of liquid forms on the beaker, and liquid starts to flow from outside to the inside. Films are formed whenever a liquid wets a surface, but the viscosity of an ordinary liquid is such that the film forms very slowly and hardly creeps. Being a superfluid, helium II forms a swiftly moving film. In (b), the flow of liquid is from inside to outside. Even if the inner vessel is raised as in (c), liquid escapes in the form of drops from the bottom!

Many questions come up. What is the order parameter? What is going on in this phase? What symmetry is broken? Is there any relationship with superconductivity? The answers are not simple, and I shall try and do what I can to explain, based on what I have discussed so far.

Box 5.1 Peter Kapitza is one of the most colourful characters in Soviet science. He was born in 1894, and studied in Leningrad. From 1916 to 1919 he was an assistant to Joffe (well known for his work on semiconductors) in the Leningrad University. In 1921 he fled to England along with his mother. There he became an assistant to Lord Rutherford at the University of Cambridge. Those were exciting years, for discovery followed discovery at Cambridge. But all this was in nuclear physics, and Kapitza did not work in this area. However, he held his own by doing brilliant work in the production of very high magnetic fields. As a result Kapitza became famous, and Rutherford established a separate lab for him. In 1934 Kapitza was invited to attend a conference in Russia but was not allowed to leave at the end of it. Rutherford did his best but could not get Kapitza back to England. Reluctantly he packed Kapitza's equipment and shipped it all to Moscow. Kapitza now established a new lab called the Institute for Physical Problems. It was here that he discovered superfluidity. During the Second World War, Kapitza used his knowledge of low temperatures to set up liquid oxygen plants needed by steel factories. When he became old, he took keen interest in education. He composed problems known as Kapitza problems which were some kind of a science quiz. The questions were interesting and also challenging. In 1977 Kapitza was awarded the Nobel Prize for his discovery of superfluidity. He died in 1984.

5.3 Symmetry breaking in liquid helium

The world we live in is really a quantum world. However, till the beginning of this century we were not aware of that because quantum effects are usually small and therefore escaped detection. There is a simple thumb rule which tells us when quantum mechanics makes its presence felt. It says that (i) the masses of the particles must be small, and (ii) the temperature must be low. The Pundits would say that I am hand waving! I certainly am, but then, physicists are known to do this sometimes.

You might say: Why does liquid helium wait till 2.2 °K to become a superfluid ? Why doesn't it do so even at 4.2 °K? That is precisely where the low temperature business comes in. You must know that the higher the temperature, the higher the kinetic energy of the atoms. When the kinetic energy is large, it interferes with quantum effects, and in liquid helium the quantum effects are able to assert themselves only below 2.2 °K. But once they take over, they really go to town. I mean, do you know that liquid helium is the only known liquid which cannot be frozen into a solid by merely lowering the temperature?

In a solid, the atoms are nicely arranged on a lattice. But when you try to do the same thing with helium atoms, they resist on account of what may be called 'quantum restlessness'. What it means is that atoms fidget. This fidgeting business is not unusual. In any solid which is at a finite temperature, there is a lot of fidgeting going on. This may be called thermal restlessness, and it disappears completely when the temperature is reduced to zero. But quantum restlessness does not, and is therefore called *zero point motion*.

In principle there is zero point motion in all solids, but in helium it is very strong since the atoms are light. Besides, they do not interact very strongly with each other. The net result is that the helium atoms simply refuse to fall in line like soldiers. Does it mean that one cannot have solid helium? Not quite – you just have to persuade the helium atoms a bit! In this case, persuasion means applying external hydrostatic pressure. If sufficient pressure is applied, then the effects of zero point motion can be overcome and solid helium *can* be produced. But release the pressure, and helium jumps back to the liquid state.

Well, that was a lengthy preamble to quantum effects in liquid helium. Do you remember what I said about quantum discipline in Chapter 4? Its time now to amplify on that. Careful experiments have shown that the way the atoms are arranged in the liquid is not altered by going below the lambda point (see Box 5.2). However, below that point, the helium atoms enter into some kind of a pact. It's as if they say: 'Listen, if somebody tries to push any one of us, we shall respond collectively'.

Let us suppose our liquid is at the absolute zero of temperature. Remember, liquid helium can do that! The liquid will then be in its lowest energy state, also called the *ground state*. In physics, words are not enough; they must be backed up with a proper mathematical description. There is a quantity called the *ground state wave function* which does this for the lowest energy state. I shall denote it by the symbol Ψ. In a manner of speaking, Ψ symbolizes the secret pact I just talked about.

Having a symbol is not enough; one should write down a formula which would explain what the symbol means. However, I shall not write down the formula since we don't need it at this stage. It is a bit complicated anyway. But I must tell you that this Ψ is a complex quantity. You must have studied complex numbers, e.g. $z = x + iy$, and stuff like that. You probably know that z can also be written as $z = re^{i\phi}$, where $r = \sqrt{(x^2 + y^2)}$ and $\phi = \tan^{-1}(y/x)$ (i.e. $\tan\phi = y/x$). The quantity ϕ is called the phase factor. There is such a phase factor hiding in the ground state wave function. So we may write,

$$\Psi = \text{Something} \times e^{i\phi}$$

Now this is interesting because the phase factor ϕ also enters the order parameter ψ for liquid helium (don't confuse Ψ and ψ !). What I mean is that the order parameter can be written as

$\psi = |\psi| e^{i\phi}$, $|\psi|$ meaning *magnitude* of ψ.

The phase factor ϕ has all the magic! You don't believe it? Just stay with me.

Let us look at symmetry breaking. The λ-transition is of second order,

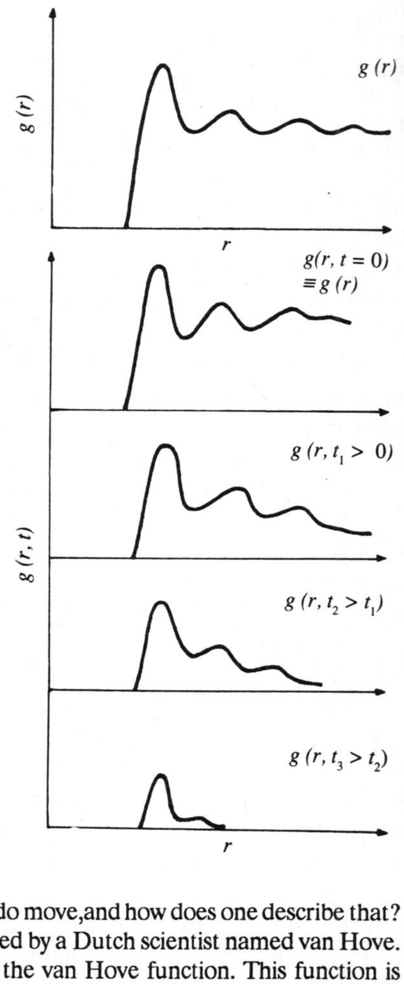

Box 5.2 In a crystal, it is easy to describe the atomic positions. One has to first define the unit cell, and then state where exactly the atoms are in the cell. If we know the atomic positions within one cell, then we know the atomic positions throughout the crystal since the latter is built up by stacking the unit cells. Finding the positions of the atoms within the unit cell is not always easy, but a good crystallographer knows how to do that. In the case of liquids, there are problems. Firstly, the atoms occupy random positions. Secondly, they move too much. So one adopts a statistical description. One introduces a *pair correlation function g(r)* defined as follows: I pick an atom at random in the liquid, and I take its centre to be the origin. I now ask: What is the probability of finding another atom at a distance *r* at the *same* instant. Notice what I am doing; I am sitting on one atom, and I am asking for the probability of finding another atom at a distance *r* at the same instant. This is like taking a group photo. X-ray diffraction enables you to take such a group photo because X-rays whizz past atoms at the speed of light and have no time to see the atoms sluggishly moving around. But the atoms do move,and how does one describe that? For that we use a function *g(r,t)* defined by a Dutch scientist named van Hove. So *g(r,t)* is sometimes referred to as the van Hove function. This function is defined as follows: I define an origin as before by selecting the centre of some arbitrary atom. I now stay put in this place even though my marker atom might drift away. This is important. So, staying put in this comfortable spot, I watch the atoms slowly move by. From time to time I measure probabilities as before; that gives me *g(r,t)*. So, *g(r,t)* is the probability of finding an atom at the point *r* at time *t*, given that there was an atom at the origin at time $t = 0$. Slow neutron scattering is used to obtain information about *g(r,t)* since neutrons, unlike X-rays are not in a hurry and manage to observe how things change with time.

OK. Why all this? Just to mention that $g(r)$ for liquid helium has been measured above and below the lambda point and it does not show a significant change, meaning that the transition does not affect the way the atoms are distributed. Some of you may be uneasy. I have been giving a classical description of $g(r)$ whereas elsewhere I am making a big pitch about quantum effects. You have a point. However, when you do an experiment, you just measure $g(r)$ as Nature has lined it up for us. The classical/quantum business enters only in the theoretical description and there you surely have to be careful!

and so we should be able to write the free energy as in eqn (3.1). Actually, I must make a small change since the order parameter is now complex. So, instead of ψ^2, I write $\psi \times \psi^*$ where ψ^* is the complete conjugate of ψ and is equal to $|\psi|e^{-i\phi}$. Hence, $\psi\psi^* = |\psi|^2$. I thus obtain

$$F = a(T - T_C)\,|\psi|^2 + b\,|\psi|^4 \tag{5.1}$$

It is interesting to look at the plots of the above equation. One expects similarities with Fig.3.2, but one also expects differences since the order parameter is complex (Fig.5.5). To represent a complex number we need a plane. And if we must plot the value of F corresponding to various points in the plane, then we obviously must go up. Thus we get free energy surfaces instead of free energy curves. Notice that these surfaces may be readily obtained by rotating the earlier curves, which is to be expected.

We now play the old game – looking for the minima. Above T_C, the minimum is always at $\psi = 0$ which means that there is no order. Below T_C, something interesting happens. Instead of just two minima as in Fig.3.1, we now have an infinite number of them distributed continuously on a circle. Each point on the circle may be identified by the corresponding value of the phase angle. There are infinite possibilities for the phase, and so helium has an infinite selection to choose from when it orders! Of course it makes only one choice – randomly.

Different values of ϕ represent different types of superfluid ordering. Suppose I have a bucket of He II described by a phase angle ϕ. If I somehow manage to change this phase to ϕ', I get a new state of ordering. The change ϕ to ϕ' is called a *gauge* transformation. What I am leading up to is the fact that the free energy (5.1) does not care what value we assign to the phase factor. This is because $\psi\psi^* = |\psi|^2$; the value of ϕ does not enter into the expression for the free energy.

So we have this important result:

The free energy is invariant under a gauge transformation, whereas the order parameter is not. So superfluidity is the result of gauge symmetry breaking.

I am sure you are quite mystified, and would like to ask: 'How do you

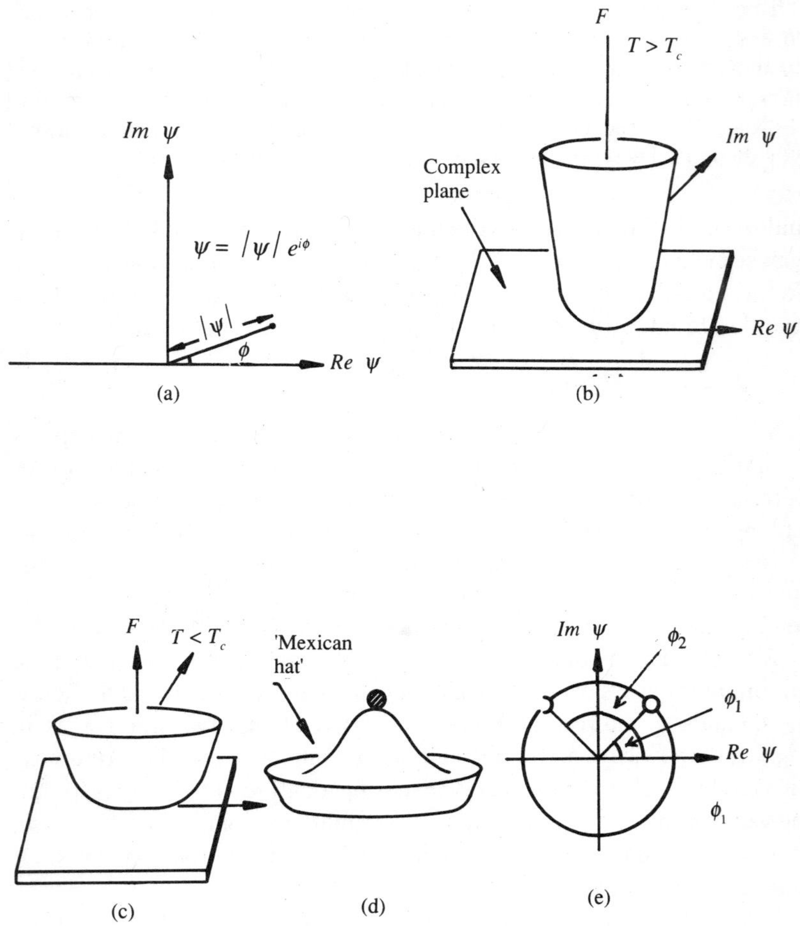

Fig.5.5 The order parameter in He II is complex. To represent the values of ψ one now requires a plane (a complex plane really as in (a)), rather than a single axis as in Fig.3.1(a). Correspondingly, the free energy is represented by a surface rather than a graph as in Fig.3.1(a). (b) and (c) show the free energy surfaces for $T > T_c$ and $T < T_c$. However, if a vertical section is made of the surface in (c) above, one would get the same sort of curves as in Fig.3.1. This is because the surfaces in the present case (see b and c) are obtained simply by rotating the old curves about the vertical axis. The bowl in (c) has an interesting shape at the bottom, and looks like a Mexican hat. It is shown separately in (d). A marble placed on top of the Mexican hat will be unstable and roll down. It can take any position along the rim, each position corresponding to a particular choice of the phase angle (see e). When liquid helium breaks gauge symmetry to become a superfluid, it acquires a particular value ϕ; the choice is random. The value of $|\psi|$ depends on temperature, and varies as in Fig.3.2.

know you are correct?' Fair enough. I must relate this ϕ-business to superfluidity. So I take a bucket of liquid helium. The phase everywhere is ϕ_1, say. Suppose I now change the phase in a small portion of the bucket to the value ϕ_2. So in part of the bucket the phase is ϕ_1 while elsewhere it is ϕ_2.

Forget superfluidity for a moment. Water flows down a mountain slope. Why? Simple, because the potential energy is lower at the bottom. In other words, water flows down the *potential energy gradient*. In a bucket of liquid helium with different phase angles in different regions, there is a phase gradient. *Superflow is caused by flow down a phase gradient*!

5.4 Superconductivity

The frictionless flow of electrons in a superconductor (see Box 5.3) has strong similarities to the superflow of He II. But, connecting the theories for the two systems is not that simple! However, if electron pairs are made in a special way, then it turns out that a collection of such electron pairs behaves rather like a collection of helium atoms in the superfluid phase. The way to form such pairs was first suggested by an American scientist named Cooper, and for this reason such pairs are often referred to as *Cooper pairs*. Later, Bardeen, Cooper and Schrieffer explained how with Cooper pairs one can have superconductivity. This was in 1958, whereas superconductivity was discovered by Kammerlingh Onnes in 1911. So for nearly half a century there was no fundamental theory of superconductivity until the famous BCS theory came along. Naturally, Bardeen and company were duly rewarded with the Nobel Prize (in 1972). This was Bardeen's second Prize in Physics, his first one being for the transistor (in 1956). He is the only person to have won the Physics Prize twice !

The BCS theory did not straightaway answer the question about the symmetry that is broken. That answer came a few years later from a bright young student in Cambridge named Josephson. This young man was attending a course of lectures given by Prof. Anderson, an American scientist. Now Anderson himself had done some work on superconductivity, and when he described his work in the class, Josephson's brain began to buzz. He kept asking: 'What is the symmetry that is broken?' Soon he reasoned that it was gauge symmetry that was broken. He showed the result to Anderson who encouraged Josephson to publish it. Josephson did, but at first many people did not believe his result, and that included the great Bardeen! However, soon many beautiful experiments were performed which proved that Josephson was right, and in 1973 he too was awarded the Nobel Prize !

How does one find the order parameter for a given transition and the symmetry that is broken? It's not always easy, and that is why I narrated the story of Josephson. Symmetry breaking is a big thing in elementary particle physics too, and here again we have the problem of identifying the symmetry that is broken. Experiments provide some clue, but one has also got to be clever!

Box 5.3 Superconductivity was initially a scientific curiosity, until people realised that it could be exploited for practical purposes. However, a major handicap was that very low temperatures were required. And so the quest began to find materials with high superconducting transition temperatures. Till 1987 the record was held by an alloy of niobium, germanium and tin with T_c ~23°K. Though this was a low temperature, people still found it worthwhile to make magnets of various niobium alloys and compounds. Remember how an electromagnet is made? You just wind a coil, and pass current through it. To get a high field, all you have to do is to (i) increase the number of turns, or (ii) increase the current. Increasing the current is not easy since it also increases the heating. In America they once had a magnet which was cooled by a small river! However, if the magnet wire is made of a superconducting material and the wire is cooled below T_c then the heat production disappears! Superconducting magnets are used in a medical equipment called NMR tomograph. A few hospitals in India have it. The maximum use of superconducting magnets is made in particle accelerators. There are such magnets all along a 28 km (circular) accelerator called LEP nearing completion in Geneva. If you think that is big, let me tell you that in America they are building an accelerator called the SSC which will have superconducting magnets all around its 85 km perimeter! (After this book was first published, the US Congress voted in 1994 to close down the SSC project as it was becoming too expensive. Even the cost of shutting down the project is astronomically high being around $600 millions! This has therefore been described as the costliest burial in history!! Particle physicists in America are most upset — naturally.) So magnets are truly big business. In India, superconducting NbTi wire has been made at the Bhabha Atomic Research Centre, and some magnets have been wound.

In 1987, the world was shaken by the news that a new superconductor had been discovered with a T_c around 40 °K. The discovery was made by Bernodz and Mueller, who later received the Nobel Prize. Previously, only metals and alloys were found to become superconducting. But Bernodz and Mueller found an oxide (an insulator) which did. Excitement swept the physics world. People dropped whatever they were doing and began to work day and night in the race to discover superconductors with higher and higher transition temperatures. Records tumbled, and there was feverish competition. Companies and governments poured money. Presidents and prime ministers headed national committees, and so on!

Why this feverish excitement? Because T_c has been pushed above the boiling point of liquid nitrogen (77°K), which meant that expensive liquid helium apparatus for maintaining superconductivity is no longer required. Superconductivity had finally become 'cheaper', and there have been forecasts of a new technological revolution.

But Nature has come in the way! The new superconducting material (a compound of yttrium, barium, copper and oxygen — formula $YBa_2Cu_3O_4$ and nicknamed yabaco) is not easily made in the form of wires. Also, its current-carrying capacity is rather small. So the companies have cooled off a bit. However, the scientists are pressing on, hoping for a breakthrough. Also, people are mystified as to how yabaco becomes superconducting. The old theories don't seem to work here.

Very recently there was news that Bell Labs (a great research laboratory which has produced many Nobelists), IBM (the computer giant) and MIT (a renowned university) have come together on the superconducting business. The details of the cooperation are a secret. It is believed that something new is going to break out — may be it will have something to do with the use of superconductors in computers!

India too has been swept by the new wave. Many groups are vigorously competing with each other, and there is healthy rivalry. For the first time, physicists in India are taking the national physics journal PRAMANA seriously, and are publishing their results in it. Why? Perhaps because PRAMANA publishes results fast, whereas foreign journals put our scientists in a long queue!

To sum up :

- Superfluidity in liquid helium is due to quantum effects.
- The quantum effects manifest in the ground state wave function.
- The ground state wave function has a phase factor which is all important.
- The same phase factor occurs also in the complex order parameter.
- Superflow occurs when there is a phase gradient.
- Gauge symmetry is broken in the superfluid transition.
- Superconductivity is due to Cooper pairs. These behave like helium atoms in the superfluid phase.
- The order parameter for the superconductor is very much like that for superfluid helium.
- Gauge symmetry is broken in the superconducting transition as well.

6 *Phase Transitions And Life*

Do phase transitions have anything to do with the origin of life? You might think this is a wild question; but the question has been asked, and it is not wild. Of course the answer is not known, but I can tell you why the question has been asked. For that I must first tell you something about *non-equilibrium phase transitions*.

6.1 Systems far from equilibrium

An equilibrium phase is characterized by well-defined values for the thermodynamic variables (see, *A Hot Story*) such as pressure, temperature, stress, etc. If the phase is an ordered one, we must add the order parameter to the list. All the transitions discussed in the previous chapters were *equilibrium* phase transitions. One variable, usually temperature, was made the *control variable*, and it was slowly varied so that at each stage the system was fully in *thermodynamic equilibrium*. What we have been discussing so far are transitions which occur during such variations of the control parameter.

Physical systems do not always have to be in thermodynamic equilibrium; in fact an example is given in Chapter 1. What I now wish to discuss is the state of a system which is driven farther and farther from equilibrium by suitably varying the control parameter (which in this case is somewhat like an applied force). Before I discuss specific examples, let us get a broad overall picture.

We start with a system in equilibrium, and slowly give increasing values to the control parameter, whatever it may be. Naturally the system would respond to this change, by going into a new state. But, if the value of the control parameter is small, the new state will be only slightly different from the original equilibrium state. For example, if we have a piece of rubber whose equilibrium shape is a cube and we squeeze it a bit, then the cube will assume a slighly different shape.

So we take this system and keep changing the control variable, driving it farther and farther away from equilibrium. We plot a graph showing the response as it varies with the control variable. The graph might look like what is shown in Fig.6.1. The initial part of the curve which grows from the state of thermodynamic equilibrium is referred to as the *thermodynamic branch*.

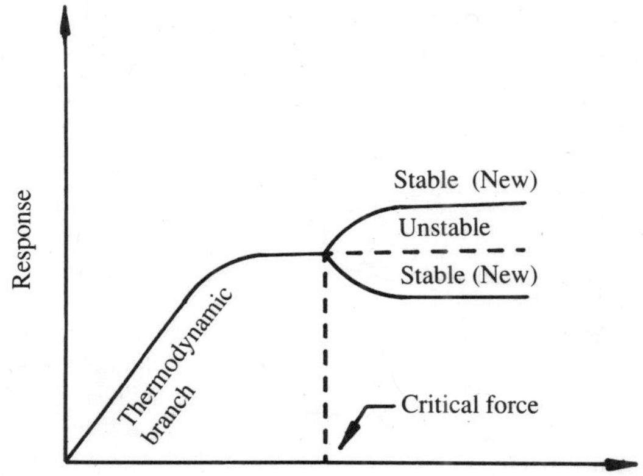

Fig.6.1 Schematic illustration of a nonequilibrium phase transition. The system is driven farther and farther away from equilibrium by a suitable external force (control parameter). The system then rides the thermodynamic branch. At a critical value of the control parameter, the thermodynamic branch becomes unstable and the system switches to a new stable branch. In the simple case illustrated here, there are two options, one of which is selected at random. The splitting shown above is sometimes referred to as *bifurcation*.

6.2 Bifurcation

Does the system ride the thermodynamic branch indefinitely? It rarely does. When the control parameter becomes sufficiently large, the thermodynamic branch usually becomes unstable while some other branch becomes stable. The system then leaves the thermodynamic branch and moves over to the new stable branch. This change over usually occurs discontinuously, and is referred to as a *nonequilibrium phase transition*.

Let us now discuss a few examples. Consider a metallic cell like the one shown in Fig.6.2. Fill it with a suitable liquid, and then close the top with a glass plate. The cell is now carefully heated from below to a temperature, say, T_2. The top is maintained at a temperature T_1 less than that of the bottom.

We have here an example of a system not in equilibrium, since the temperature is not the same everywhere. So how does the system respond? Have you heard of convection or the circulation of a fluid due to temperature variations? That's what happens now. The fluid at the bottom is hotter and lighter; so it rises to the top. The liquid at the top is colder and heavier; so it moves towards the bottom.

Going back to Fig.6.2, here $\Delta T = T_2 - T_1$, is the control variable. As T_2 is raised, i.e. as $\Delta T = (T_2 - T_1)$, the temperature difference is increased, the convection becomes more and more vigorous. But it is also pretty disorganised. However, when ΔT is increased beyond a critical value (this depends on the fluid, the shape of the vessel and maybe a

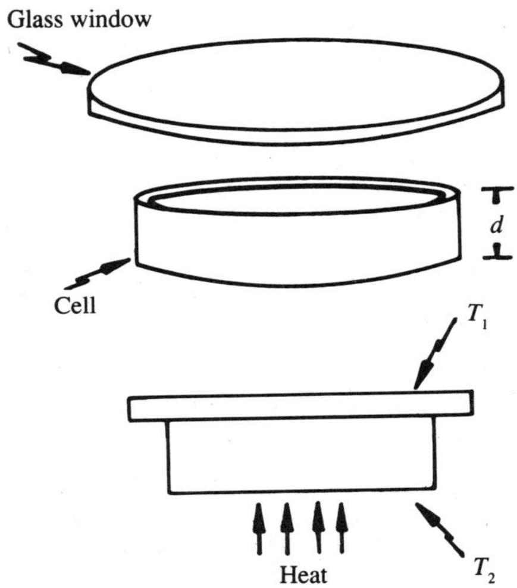

Fig.6.2 Arrangement used for demonstrating convection instabilities. The fluid is held in a metallic cell covered at the top with a glass plate to permit viewing. The cell is heated from below. To facilitate the observation of the convection patterns, aluminium powder is sprinkled into the cell. The cell geometry can be either circular as above or rectangular. The spacing *d* is much smaller than the lateral dimensions.

couple of other things), something spectacular happens, i.e. the convection becomes ordered, leading to geometrical patterns as in Fig.6.3. A 2-dimensional lattice structure has developed, and in fact it even has a (topological) defect! Figure 6.4 shows other convection patterns. It is possible to explain the pattern of Fig.6.3 along the lines illustrated in Fig.6.5. But even so, the lattice structure is remarkable. Who would have thought that such a thing is possible? Such things happen because Nature is often lazy (!) and tends to imitate herself. This is a useful thing to remember.

6.3 Concerning patterns

The patterns in Figs.6.3 and 6.4 are frozen, i.e. they do not vary in time; they are purely *spatial* patterns. Sometimes one can have *temporal* patterns, i.e. patterns with time variations. There are some chemicals which, if you mix in a test tube say, react with each other and produce beautiful colours. At any given time the mixture has only one colour, but the colours vary with time. This is a case of a temporal pattern. The laser is another good example: it emits a light wave of a well-defined frequency. The most

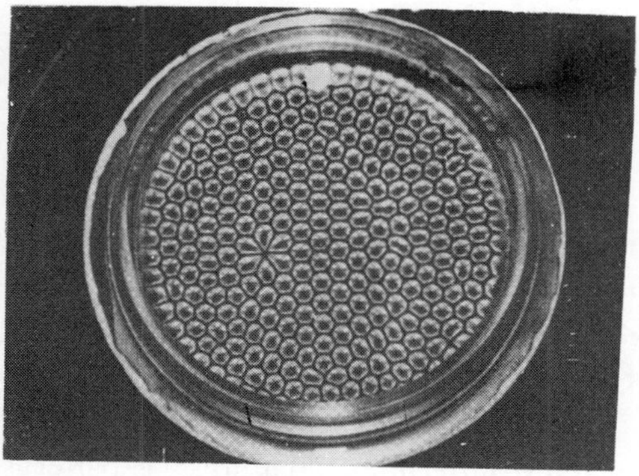

Fig.6.3 Hexagonal convection cells in silicone oil. Notice the defect.

Fig.6.4 Some other examples of convection patterns.

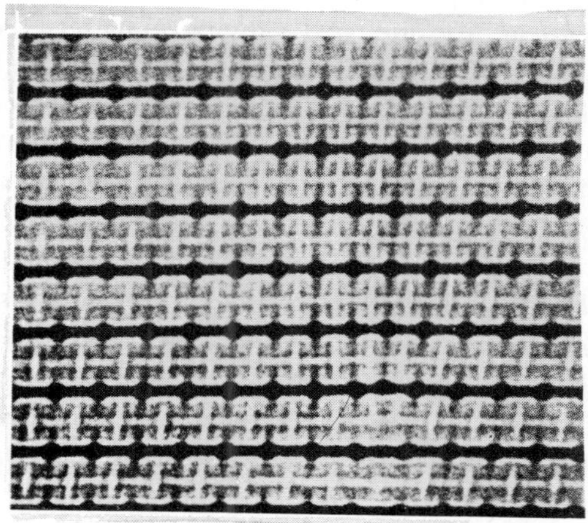

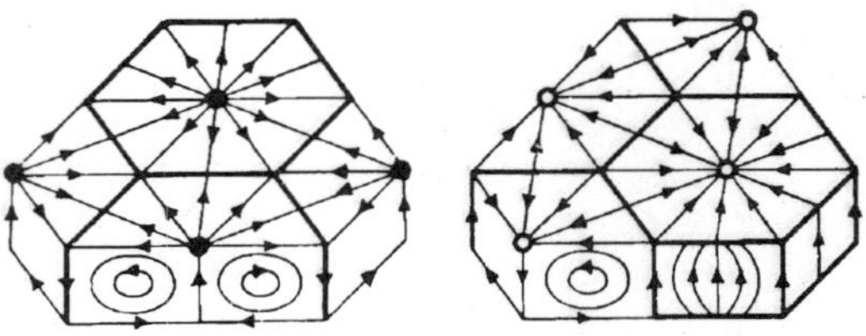

Fig.6.5 This figure illustrates the formation of hexagonal cells. There are two types of cells. In one the liquid flows away from the centre, while in the other the liquid flows towards the centre.

complex situation is where one has *spatio-temporal* patterns, i.e. patterns which vary both in space and in time. Some reactions called *rotating chemical reactions* do this; they are spectacular.

Thus when the system leaves the thermodynamic branch, the stable state it acquires may be associated with a spatial pattern or a temporal pattern or even a spatio-temporal pattern. How does one describe this change of branch? Is there a quantity like the free energy we had before? If not, what do we do? Well, in some cases there is a quantity like our free energy, but Prof. Haken of Germany has shown that we don't really need such a quantity. One has simply to formulate an equation which describes what happens to the system under the action of the applied force. The solution of this equation will give the stable state under the conditions of the applied force. Of course, to formulate such an equation one must understand the process (e.g. convection) properly, but once that is done, the job is one of solving the equation. Haken himself has suggested many tricks and if they are not enough one could always look through mathematical literature to see if someone else has done something similar elsewhere.

Thanks to Haken's initiative, the study of patterns is now big business, and people have even figured out how such patterns are formed on shells. But don't think that everything has been done. The patterns in Nature are too numerous to be exhausted that easily! Is there a basic reason why such patterns occur? Yes there is, and that is connected with nonlinearities. This is a bit involved, and we will not go into it here. You might like to look at Box 4.1 where I have mentioned nonlinearities.

6.4 Symmetry breaking aspects

The beautiful patterns must have made you wonder about symmetry breaking. Does symmetry breaking operate in nonequilibrium phase transitions? It does, though in a slightly different manner. Earlier, I compared the symmetry group of the free energy with that of the ordered state. As I mentioned, in the case of nonequilibrium transitions, one works with an equation (like the one proposed by Haken). This equation has invariances (remember my earlier remark about symmetry of equations?), and we compare these with the symmetries of the *stable solution* of these system of equations, corresponding to the value under consideration of the control parameter. The solution corresponding to the thermodynamic branch will have the same symmetry as that of the parent equation, but the solution that is selected after bifurcation will usually have less symmetry. So one can talk of symmetry breaking in this case also.

6.5 Origin of life

I now come to the difficult question about the origin of life, and its possible relation to phase transitions. Before I tackle these, I must say a few words about what scientists generally feel about the origin of life. Without getting mixed up with religious questions, most scientists believe that it must be possible to explain the origin of life on earth by the laws of physics and chemistry.

The very first living objects that appeared did not have eyes, ears and things like that. They were quite simple, much simpler than even the (biological) cell we are familiar with today. What this ancestor of ours was we don't exactly know, but we do know that this creature was nothing more than a big molecule; however, it was a most unusual molecule compared to anything that existed earlier.

What did this molecule consist of, and where did it appear from? There are good reasons to believe that in those days (about $\sim 10^9$ years ago), a good portion of the earth was covered with water containing, among other substances, amino acids and other proteins, out of which biological molecules are built (see Fig. 6.6 and Box 6.1). This sea is sometimes referred to as the *prebiotic soup*. Careful experiments (particularly by the Sinhalese scientist Ponnamperuma) to simulate the conditions of those days have demonstrated beyond doubt that something like the prebiotic soup must have existed. Floating in this soup were all the building blocks of larger biological molecules. But no biological molecule existed until somehow, sometime, these building blocks combined together to make our great, great ... grandfather (a super molecule really) who behaved as if he had life!

What is life? The great physicist Erwin Schrodinger (who won the Nobel Prize for his discovery of wave mechanics) once said: 'Living matter evades decay to equilibrium'. We can translate it as: A living object is in a state far from equilibrium. If that object attains thermodynamic equilibrium, then it is dead! So we have a new definition of death – a physicist's definition.

Let us go back to the living world. The Soviet scientist and academician

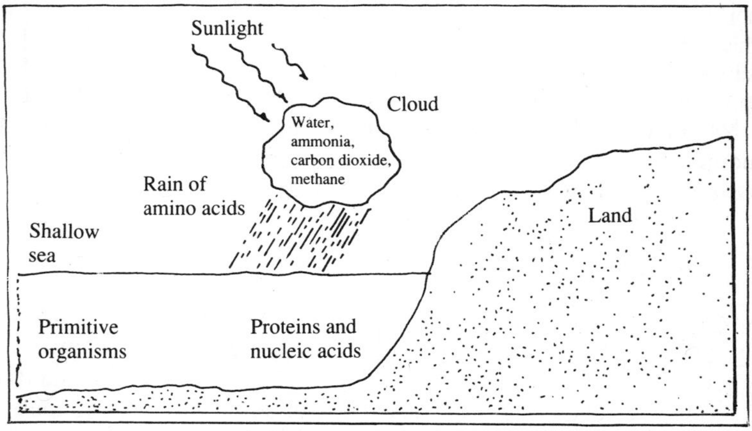

Fig.6.6 Ultraviolet light from the young Sun caused electrical discharges in the atmosphere (which then had a lot of methane) producing amino acids, which then came down along with rain. Ponnamperuma has demonstrated with suitable experiments that amino acids could have been formed in this manner. In the seas and shallow lagoons of those days, these acids kept on combining in various ways most of which resulted in molecules that were inert. One combination however became selfreplicating, signalling the origin of life on Earth. Could there be planets of other stars in the Universe where this sort of thing could have happened? Why not? Will there be 'litle green men' in those planets? We don't know. Can we communicate with them? People think so. Think about it!

Oparin (who won the Kalinga award for popular science writing in 1977) has given us three rules which must be obeyed by a system to qualify for being termed a living system.

1. It must exhibit metabolism. That is, it must supply itself energy by taking molecules from outside, combining them suitably, absorbing what is needed, and rejecting the waste. To put it simply, the system must be able to feed!
2. The system must be able to reproduce.
3. It must be capable of undergoing mutation.

Every living thing we can think of, satisfies these criteria.

Conditions were not static in the prebiotic soup – the concentration of the ingredient molecules must have been changing, the temperature must have been changing and so on. At some time, the conditions must have been just right for our ancestor to have been born and from then on there has been no looking back. What I mean is that the control parameters might have assumed a value when the 'living molecule' represented a stable state, and Nature promptly seized that opportunity.

Box 6.1 Proteins are high molecular weight organic compounds composed mainly of C, H, O, and N but possibly also containing some P and S. Keratin which makes up our skin and collagen which is found in our muscles are examples of proteins. All proteins are built up from amino acids (like glycine, alanine, lysine, etc.). In all, 26 amino acids exist but only 20 occur regularly.

You must have heard of the DNA. It is perhaps the most famous of the nucleic acids. The basic building blocks of the nucleic acids are just four: Adenine (A), Thymine (T), Guanine (G), and Cytosine (C). In the DNA there are two sugar phosphate chains twisting around like a stair case, the steps of which are made up by nucleic acid base pairs as shown in the figure. The interesting thing is that A will combine only with T and G with C. The DNA structure is referred to as the double helix. Watson (who discovered this structure along with Crick for which they received the Nobel Prize) has described the thrilling story of the discovery in his book *The Double Helix*. You **must** read it!

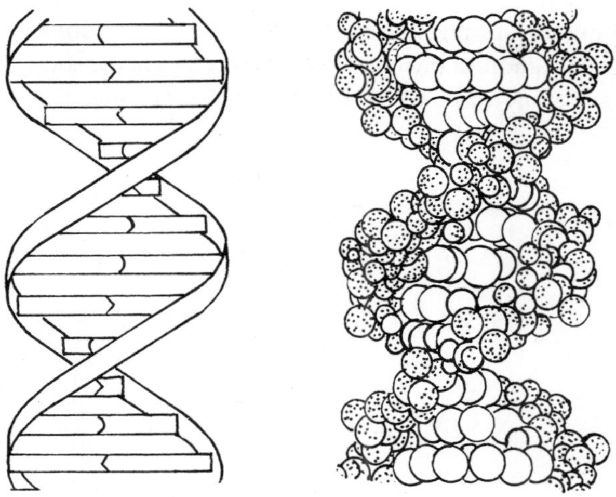

Sounds like hand waving? Well it is, up to a point but not quite. One could make a detailed mathematical model and check it all out to some extent. Checking means making proper and realistic assumptions about the molecular species that must have existed then, their concentrations in the soup, their reaction rates, etc. One must see if the model leads to a nonequilibrium phase transition, and whether the new stable state has the properties Oparin has specified. Prof. Eigen in Germany is doing work of this kind. Some supporting experimental work is also going on.

As I said earlier, we do not have the answers at present, but we at least know how to proceed. I should mention that a few years ago, there were a couple of conferences in India on the Origin of Life. Physicists can't work on this sort of thing by themselves; they have to work in collaboration with chemists and biologists. In other words, this is an interdisciplinary subject.

To sum up:

- Systems driven far from equilibrium seek new stable states.
- These states usually have spatial and/or temporal ordering.
- The jump to such new states can be visualised as a nonequilibrium phase transition.
- The transition can be analysed by setting up a suitable equation and solving it.
- The ordering present in the new states could be viewed in terms of symmetry breaking.
- The origin of life (in the prebiotic soup) could be viewed as a nonequilibrium phase transition associated with complex chemical reactions amongst the constituent molecules in the soup, and leading to a super molecule which behaved as if it had life.

7 *Phase Transitions And The Early Universe*

Do phase transitions have anything to do with the origin of the Universe? If the question asked at the beginning of Chapter 6 seemed wild, this one must appear even wilder. However, one can answer this question with a 'yes' with greater confidence than perhaps in the earlier case. How is that? Well, let me try and explain.

7.1 The expanding Universe

Our Universe is awfully big. The farthest galaxies are at least a billion light years away. You must be knowing what a light year is. It is the distance that light travels in one year. In one second, light travels 3×10^5 kilometres. So 10^9 light years is a mighty long distance. Our Universe is not only big, but is also *expanding*. This means that tomorrow it will be bigger than it is today. In the same way, it is bigger today than it was yesterday and so on. If we keep going further back in time in this manner, then a stage will be reached when the Universe was not all that big. In fact it would have been no more than a tiny speck! But for that we have to go back about 15 billion years or so. By the way, when I say the Universe was tiny once upon a time, I do not mean that all the matter in the Universe was packed into one tiny spot in a space that was otherwise vast and empty. Rather space (or space-time as Einstein would have it) was itself tiny! An expanding Universe can be understood by imagining the Universe to be like a balloon that is being inflated. Assume the balloon started off from a point size, and think of its surface area as being approximately the size of the Universe. This gives you some sort of a mental picture (but don't push the analogy too hard!)

You may say, 'Hold on. How do you know that once upon a time the Universe was really tiny? Couldn't we have an evolution like in Fig.7.1(b)?' Good question! There is strong experimental evidence to believe that our Universe originated in a Big Bang billions of years ago, and that our Universe then had a radius of less than about 10^{-48}cm!

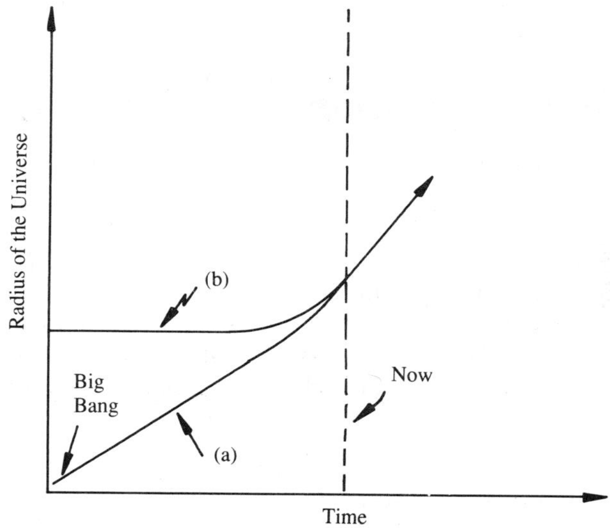

Fig.7.1 Scenarios for the evolution of our Universe (schematic)! We assume it is spherical and plot its radius as a function of time. Curve (a) shows the time-variation if the Universe originated in a Big Bang. Curve (b) shows another possibility where, for some reason or the other, the Universe which was quite steady, began to expand. Today we see this expansion going on, but in the distant past the Universe could have been steady. The discovery of Penzias and Wilson has ruled out curve (b).

Unfortunately, today's theories cannot really say what happened when the Universe was smaller than this size. Does it all sound incredible? Well, that is Nature in one word!

7.2 The Big Bang

So there was this tiny speck a long time ago, with a tremendous amount of energy and/or matter (remember, $E = mc^2$ means that matter and energy are equivalent) packed into it. You know what happens if too much energy is packed into too little a volume; there is an explosion. That is the Big Bang which gave birth to our Universe which we now see as being so big and so full of stars. Don't ask what existed before the Big Bang! That is a good question though; maybe I will answer it elsewhere.

The first few minutes of the Universe were really hectic and very eventful. Lots of things happened in a twinkle, and the famous physicist Steven Weinberg (about whom I shall shortly say something more) has written a fascinating book called *The First Three Minutes* about the wav our Universe was born. You should read it.

You ask, 'How do you know there was a Big Bang?' Well, there is tell-tale evidence. You go to a friend's house on Deepavali day. You see lots of torn pieces of paper lying around, and you know right away that your friend has been firing crackers. You guessed that from the **remnants** of the explosion. Similarly, scientists detected the remnants of the Big Bang. This discovery was quite accidental. Two scientists named Penzias and Wilson working in the famous Bell Laboratories of America were setting up an antenna for some satellite communication work. This was in the early sixties. Their antenna was very sensitive, and kept on detecting a background noise – a radio hiss you might call it. This hiss was heard no matter in which direction the antenna was pointed. Many careful experiments were then performed, and the following conclusions were reached.

1. The radio noise was like heat radiation coming from a hot plate.
2. The radiation corresponded to a temperature of about 3 °K.
3. This 'cosmic noise' originated during the Big Bang.

The Big Bang is thus an experimentally established fact. There are also models of cosmology (this is the name given to the study of the Universe) which support the Big Bang idea. Now comes the problem of reconstructing the events during the Big Bang. This is like describing what happens inside a cracker when the gunpowder is burning and the cracker is beginning to explode. To describe those historic moments, we must turn to elementary particle physics.

7.3 Unification of forces

You must have heard that there are only four basic forces in Nature (see Box 7.1). These are,

1. the *gravitational force* discovered by Newton,
2. the *electromagnetic force* about which we learnt through the discoveries of Coulomb, Ampere, Faraday and Maxwell,
3. the *weak force* that controls radioactivity and explained to us by E.C.G.Sudarshan, and also by Gell-Mann and Feynman,
4. the *strong force* that binds neutrons and protons inside the nuclei.

Besides the four basic forces, there are a host of so-called elementary particles – electron, positron, proton, neutron and so on. So, there are these particles, and there are these forces. The Sun, the Moon, the stars, you and me, everything around us is the result of a complicated mixture of these basic building blocks, i.e. the basic forces and the elementary particles.

Box 7.1 The four fundamental forces are: (i) the gravitational force, (ii) the weak force, (iii) the electromagnetic force, and (iv) the strong force. Often the word 'interaction' is used instead of the word 'force'. Where exactly these forces operate has been explained in the text. They differ in two important respects, namely, range and strength. You already know (see Box 1.3) that both the gravitational and the electromagnetic interaction vary as $1/r$. It means that both these interactions do not vanish even if r is very large — the magnitude of the interaction may be very very small but it does **not** vanish; that is the important point. By contrast, both the strong and the weak interactions vanish or become zero when the distance r (between the interacting objects) exceeds, say, 10^{-12} cm. In other words, gravitational and electromagnetic interactions are *long-ranged*, while the other two are *short-ranged*. See figure below. It is indeed remarkable that Nature has four forces, two of which reach out to the farthest corners of the Universe, while the remaining two do not extend beyond microscopic distances.

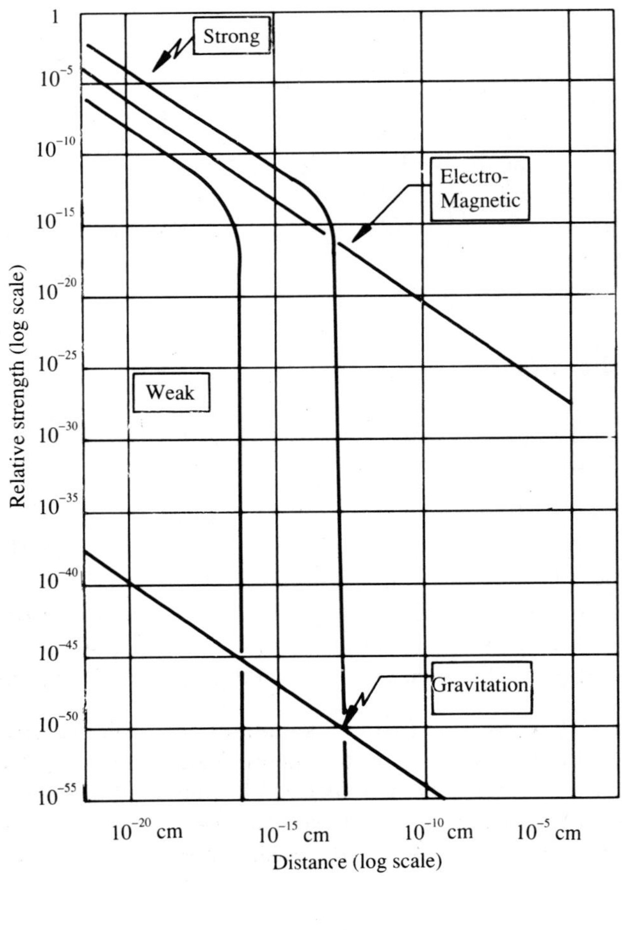

What about strength? Consider two electrons distance r apart. The gravitational and the electrostatic interactions between the two are given respectively by

$$V_G = (Gm^2)/r$$

and

$$V_{EM} = (e^2)/r$$

Now take the ratio V_G / V_{EM} and put in the numbers. The distance r gets cancelled out and you will get $Gm^2/e^2 \sim 10^{-40}$. This shows roughly how much weaker gravitation is compared to the electromagnetic force. The strength of a force is measured in terms of a quantity called the *coupling constant*. If we make a (relative) ladder of strength, we then get roughly the following:

Strong	1
Electromagnetic	10^{-2}
Weak	10^{-5}
Gravitational	10^{-40}

Observe that the gravitational force is even feebler than the so-called weak force! But because of its long range, it has a big say in shaping our Universe.

One question which has puzzled scientists for many years is: Why are there only four basic forces? Are they related to each other? Are they all descended from one parent force, some kind of a *unified* force?

The search for the unification of forces is a great passion with physicists. The great Einstein started it all. He tried to unify gravity and the electromagnetic force. He tried for several years, but did not succeed. We now know why he failed, but nevertheless, everybody continues to admire Einstein for his courage and determination. Although Einstein himself failed, his quest for unification has inspired many others.

In the early seventies, Abdus Salam, Weinberg and Glashow showed that the weak and the electromagnetic forces could be unified into one thing called the *electro-weak force*. How do we know this is true? Experiments of course. If one does experiments at sufficiently high energies, then one finds many things that a unified, electro-weak theory would predict (maybe, I will write a book on this someday!). Such experiments are both difficult and costly, and require very high-energy accelerators.

Once the electro-weak unification idea was verified, people tried very hard to rope in the strong interaction also. The theory which marries the strong force to the electro-weak force is popularly referred to as the *Grand Unification Theory* (GUT). At present we do not know for sure whether GUT is true or not. One day experiments will reveal the truth, but meanwhile one believes that grand unification is possible. That leaves the gravity fellow. He is much harder to rope in, but imaginative minds are already at work.

You must have noticed that unification occurs only as one goes higher and higher in energy. It is like in a big river. Just before the river enters the sea, it splits into many small streams which together make up the delta. But if you go away from the sea and up the delta, you will observe the streams all linking up one by one, till you see the big river from which they were all born. It is the same way with the fundamental forces; the higher the energy, the more unified they appear.

How much energy is required for all *four* forces to be unified? An awful lot of energy, which we can never produce in the laboratory. But

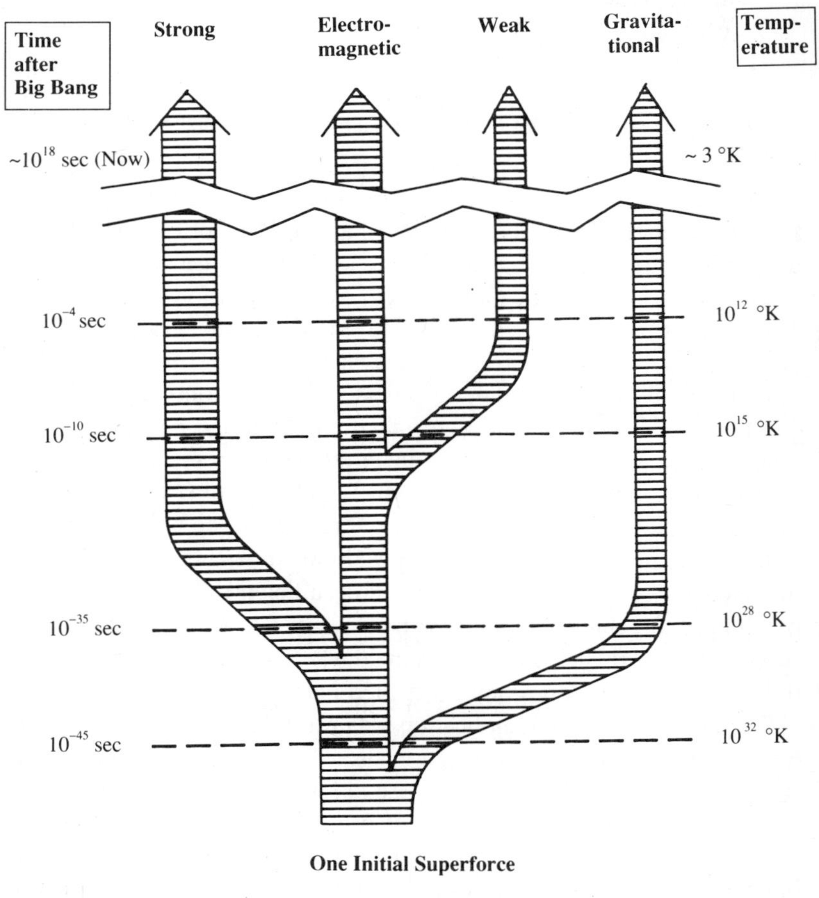

Fig.7.2 Breaking up of the original unified force into its four components in the early Universe. Notice how quickly this break-up occurred. It is believed that every peel-off could be likened to a phase transition.

such energies existed in the early Universe, and so at that time there must have been a remarkable unification. As the Universe evolved, the forces split and peeled off like the streams in a river delta — see Fig.7.2. and Box 7.1.

7.4 Phase transitions and unification

Now comes the phase transition idea. The details are quite involved, and, to be honest, I don't understand all of it myself! But the basic idea is simple and relates easily to what we learnt before. You must have heard the word *field*, as in electric field, magnetic field, gravitational field and so forth. Many particle physicists swear by fields, not just the above fields, but some basic field. And like magic, they try to pull everything out of this field! I mean all the elementary particles, the forces — the whole works really.

Of course you can't do all this with words. You must have maths. When you do the maths, field is described by a variable ϕ, rather like our old friend ψ. One now asks two questions:

1. How does the energy density depend on ϕ at a given temperature ?
2. What is the state of the field corresponding to the minimum energy?

By the way, our Universe was pretty hot in the beginning, and cooled off as time went on. Hence I am bringing in temperature. Some scenarios for the energy density are shown in Fig.7.3 and they must be familiar. It is believed that as the Universe began to cool down, the energy density

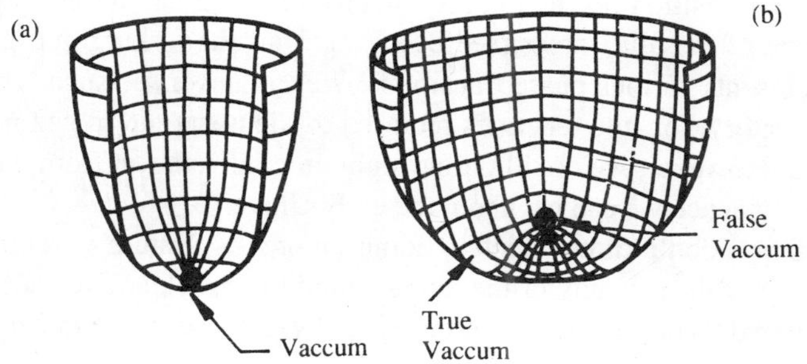

Fig.7.3 Some scenarios for the field density in the early moments after the Big Bang. Above a critical temperature T_C, there is only one minimum or 'vacuum' (see a). When the temperature decreases below T_C, the field density assumes the shape of a Mexican hat — recall Fig.5.5. The Universe then at first finds itself in a 'false vacuum' but then jumps from the 'false' to the 'true' vaccum causing a phase transition as in (b). Notice the Mexican hat structure of the bottom. Accompanying each such jump or phase transition is the birth of a new force — peeling off, if you like, as in the previous figure. When a force is born, the corresponding particles also appear.

Box 7.2 This explanation must appear like the waving of ten pairs of hands! I wouldn't blame you if you thought so. After all these concepts are highly technical, and must be described in the language best suited for them namely, mathematics. But alas, all that is pretty highbrow stuff. Even so, there is no harm in using words to describe the central idea.

In the Universe as we presently see it, we can make a distinction between particles and energy. Of course the two are interconvertible in a sense. However, at the instant of creation, (we think) there was only energy, resident in what is called a field. If you wish, this field is like the prebiotic soup of the last Chapter. Everything is pulled out of it so to speak. It is this field which is portrayed in Fig.7.3.

The state of lowest energy of the field is called *vacuum*. Don't confuse this vacuum with what we can produce by suction! A phase transition involves a jump from an 'unphysical' to a physical vacuum. This happens when temperature changes. It is believed that there was one such jump every time a force peeled off. Once a force appeared on the scene, so did the distinctive particles associated with it. For example, when the electromagnetic and the weak forces separated, photons, the quanta of the electromagnetic field, appeared on the scene.

All this must sound pretty bewildering. Indeed it is. But it is not all idle speculation. Every idea is backed by calculations, the results of which can be tested with experiments or other cross checks. This way, the plausible is separated from the implausible. The process goes on. We haven't understood everything, but we are much better informed than we were, say fifty years ago.

started varying as shown in Fig.7.3. Naturally there were phase transitions, and every transition resulted in a symmetry breaking and a related peeling off of one of the four forces (see Box 7.2). Thus the forking in Fig.7.2 really represents various phase transitions. We can never see such forking in the laboratory, for the energies required to demonstrate it can never be attained. However, we could perhaps obtain confirmation from whatever tell-tale evidence we can get about the early Universe.

Frankly, I don't know which to admire more — Nature's cleverness in packaging or the capacity of the human mind to unpack and reveal! I leave you to wonder, and will not spoil the effect by attempting a summary.

8 *Some Parting Thoughts*

So what do you think of all this? You must spend some time pondering about all that you have read. From my side, I would like to say a few things.

Many young people think that elementary particles are the only things worth studying in physics. This is a mistake for several reasons. Firstly, even if one knows all about the fundamental forces, it does not help to explain why water freezes. One could be snooty and say, 'I am not concerned', but that would be foolish. Our understanding of Nature would be incomplete if we tried to explain only some things and not others.

The study of the collective (statistical) behaviour of a large number of particles is an important branch of physics known as *many-body physics*. To do many-body physics, one must know how particles in the system interact with each other. This is like knowing the fundamental forces. That is just the starting point. Afterwards, one has to do a lot of work before one can explain things like phase change, symmetry breaking, etc. Demonstrating these things is far from trivial. As Prof. Anderson of America puts it: 'More is different'. Also, it can be rewarding — at least it was for Wilson, for it won for him the Nobel Prize; and so also for Landau, Anderson and several others.

Actually, in many respects, the dividing line between many-body physics and elementary particle physics is quite thin these days. In fact, the idea of symmetry breaking which particle physicists are so fond of using, found application first in condensed matter physics (that is the new fashionable name for the good old solid and liquid state physics!).

This brings me to the next thing I wanted to say. There are two questions you should always ask yourself: 'What are the unsolved problems in this area?' Maybe everything interesting has already been done. In that case you should ask the second question. 'Can these ideas be applied elsewhere?' People often don't ask this question, but the smart ones do! And when they do, they often open up new avenues.

The work of de Gennes (another Nobel laureate) on liquid crystals provides a classic example. For many years he worked on superconductivity. And then one fine day he said: 'I have had enough of this superconductivity. Let me now go on to something else.' And so he moved on to liquid crystals. At that time he knew very little about liquid crystals, but he did not spend years reading all there is to know about liquid crystals (this is a mistake which people often make!) Instead he did just a bit of reading, talked to a lot of people who worked on liquid crystals (this is important, i.e. discussions) and said: 'Well, I know a few tricks which I picked up while studying superconductors. Let me see if I can use them'. He could, and all of a sudden, liquid crystals became a fashionable subject!

Some years later, de Gennes did a similar switch. This time he jumped to polymers, again making it a fashionable subject. Of course people like de Gennes are not common, but that is not the point. The point is that tricks learnt in one place can be applied elsewhere. And there are many examples to prove this. One must make the attempt of course!

Always remember one thing – Nature is pretty lazy! You might not be aware of it, but she could be using the same rules in some unfashionable area as she is in a fashionable one like particle physics. Of course she is very clever and will not easily let you know this. But once you discover similarities, you have the upper hand so to speak. You may even find that particle physics and polymers are neighbours. No, I am not kidding. There are some French physicists who actually publish papers both on polymers and elementary particles. Honest!

So try to overcome any preconceived notions you might have and learn to admire Nature in all her aspects. If you dig deep enough, you will see a beautiful similarity between many subjects. You must develop the ability to uncover the similarities, and then stand back to admire what you have discovered. Then you can have all the fun you want. Guaranteed!

Suggestions for further reading

This and other books in this series can be read by themselves. However, many have expressed the feeling that I should offer some suggestions for further reading. This is not as simple a task as it might appear at first. Nevertheless, let me do the best I can. I must add that in preparing the list given below, I have benefited much from the advice of Professor V. Balakrishnan.

The books listed below do not all deal with the topic of the present volume, but there are linkages.

1. Dawkins, R. *The Selfish Gene*, Oxford University Press : New York, 1976.
2. Dmitriev, I. S. *Symmetry in the World of Molecules*, Mir Publishers: Moscow, 1979.
3. Dyson, F. J. *Origins of Life*, Cambridge University Press : Cambridge, 1985.
4. Eigen, M., Gardiner, W., Schuster, P. and Winckler-Oswatitch, R. '*The Origin of Genetic Information*,' Scientific American, 244(4):88 1981.
5. Ginzburg, V. L. *Key Problems in Physics and Astrophysics*, Mir Publishers: Moscow, 1984.
6. Jayaraman, A. '*The Diamond Anvil High-Pressure Cell*,' Scientific American, 250(4) : 42–50, 1984.
7. Kitaigorodsky, A. I. *Order and Disorder in the World of Atoms*, Mir Publishers: Moscow, 1980.
8. Leggett, A. J. *The Problems of Physics*, Oxford University Press: Oxford, 1987.
9. Lifshitz, E. M. '*Superfluidity*,' Scientific American, 198(6):30, 1958.
10. Prigogene, I. and Stagers, I. *Order out of Chaos*, Heinemann: London,1984.
11. Smordinsky, Ya. A. *Temperature*, Mir Publishers: Moscow, 1984.
12. Watson, J. D. *The Double Helix*, Signet Books: New York, 1969.
13. Wilson, K. G. '*Problems in Physics with Many Scales of Length*,' Scientific American, 244(8): 140, 1979.

Index

Note: Page numbers in brackets refer to illustrations.